...And Mistakes Made Along the Way

A Memoir by Fred Beauford

Prologue, who am I

Most people hate to admit to mistakes, especially the personal kind which could call into question the very essence of who they are, and how their personhood measures up to others. They have learned the hard lesson that others are just waiting to pounce, with unforgivable ferocity, when they point out a personal lapse in good judgment on their part: "Oh no, I must say, with no disrespect intended, but even you must admit that that was pretty dumb. That wouldn't have been me. I learned long ago not to do something so obviously foolish."

Ouch, and double ouch!

Speaking of the obvious, it is quite apparent from a statement like that, that we human beings obviously love one-upping each other and casting our own fragile existence in the most favorable light—auteur filmmakers of our own lives, if you will.

So why give anyone the clear, obvious opening by confessing to fallibility, and revealing a "dumb" self one would be better served to conceal.

Yet, in this memoir, which will recount aspects of my long, and yet, surprisingly, short stay on earth, I will give example after example of myself displaying rank ignorance, wide-eyed naivety and just plain willful foolishness.

I was inspired to write this book for many reasons. For one, I have that one thing that will inspire any writer: a willing publisher, and the fact that I own the publishing company, along with my brother. This is a far cry from the begging and groveling I had to go through when I first started writing in 1997, before I took matters into my own hands.

A book I read also inspired me. After the publication of my novel *The King Of Macy's*, the question then became, what's next? I no longer had an excuse not to write. It didn't hurt that I now wrote a book column and knew intimately what the major houses were publishing. Soon, out of the large numbers of books I received daily, one stuck out.

So, I took my own best advice and picked up Leo Damrosch's *Jean-Jacques Rousseau: Restless Genius*. When I was a university professor teaching creative writing, I would often advise my students that when they were in a deep funk and feeling as if none of it made any sense, or that they would ever get anywhere in such a strange field—not to read the works of famous writers, but instead, to read their biographies. (I deliberately recommended biographies over autobiographies, because writers, especially the creative types, tend to lie a lot!).

I made my recommendation because I knew they would see the ups and downs, the total despair and self-doubt, the never ending rejections, and the occasional triumphs that are part of almost every serious writer's career. They would see that some famous writers such as Herman Melville and Zora Neale Hurston, died broke and obscure, total failures, only to be discovered years later, lionized, and become a part of the world's literary canon, as they well deserved; or like the great Langston Hughes, who wrote his best poem, "*The Negro Speaks of Rivers*" when he was only nineteen, and was never able to top himself, yet was still the first black man in America to make a living almost solely off of his writings.

Or the numbers of writers, from D.H. Lawrence, to Mark Twain, Walt Whitman, Henry Miller, and Allen Ginsberg, to name a few, who had to self-publish, publish abroad, or publish with obscure publishers.

All of this recommended reading was meant to give them insight into what it means to be a writer, and for them not to despair at small, or large, setbacks and slights, or see themselves solely as a black, white, woman, Jewish, or gay writer, but instead as a part of a brave, noble continuum; one writer after another, male and female, straight or gay, religious or non-religious-- all the races of the earth, slowly building on a long, world-wide tradition which speaks to that which is most human in all of us.

And sure enough, there it all was in Damrosch's *Jean-Jacques Rousseay:Restless Genius* artfully laid out in black and white: a restless youth, motherless, with a father who sent him away at an early age, someone unable to hold a job, thought of as someone who had no ideas of his own, self-educated, socially inept, and had failed sexual relationships with women. In fact, it was only around page 200 in a 494 page book, when Rousseau was in his thirties, that he finally wrote something worthwhile.

This was at a time when most people were dead by forty.

Of course, as you literary types well know, he went on to arguably become one of France's greatest writers, and one of the world's most well known authors. His ideas, and his greatest literary invention, and greatest gift to us, is the modern autobiography. His Confessions depicted the individual for the first time as a unique, special creature, one who takes center stage over God. (it seems that actors and sports stars have taken the place of God as far as most modern American publishers are concerned).

I am not claiming to be the American Rousseau (although I do have a French last name). I wouldn't reject the honor, either, because I soon saw myself on the pages of Damrosch's excellent book.

I soon found myself unable to put the book down, and found myself cheering Rousseau on, hardly able to wait to turn the pages because I knew he would ultimately triumph.

So, with Rousseau's example in mind, I began this book.

November19,2005,12:05pm

Border'sBookStore,ThirdFloor

ThirdStreetPromenade

Santa Monica, CA.

Chapter One--
The Morton's of Virginia

The first memory that I remember clearly was living with a woman named Mrs. Jones. I can't picture her in my mind. I don't know if she was young or old, lived alone or with a husband, was fair skin or was as black as the ace of spades. I just know that I lived there in her house with my two brothers, and we often played a game we called "blackout."

We would make the sound of loud sirens going off, and jump up on the bed and pull the shades down, or cover the windows with whatever we could find. I had no idea why we were playing such a game. In the rank ignorance of a four-year-old, how was I supposed to know that I was living in coastal Asbury Park, New Jersey, in 1944, and everyone, young and old, played "blackout." The grown-ups, however, played it with a deadly seriousness, with real sirens going off, afraid that one day it wouldn't be role playing at all, but that the Germans or the Japanese were really overhead, ready to bomb them out of existence.

But, just as the picture of living with Mrs. Jones started becoming clearer, and was beginning to fix itself permanently in my mind with this strange thing we call memory, without any warning that I know of, I found myself, along with by two brothers, pulling up in a taxi to a large white house in Northern Virginia. Standing in the yard to greet us was a friendly looking, fair skinned older woman who looked a lot like the woman who came and took us away from Mrs. Jones, and called herself our mother.

It was my first introduction to the world of the Morton's of Virginia.

Our mother only stayed with us for a few days and was gone, to where I did not know, and strangely, if I remember correctly, did not care. We didn't see her again for almost two years.

Life on the big farm with my grandparents was a grand adventure. Now, both as an emotionally detached historian with a detailed knowledge of American history, and as the equally detached novelist with an ability to silently eavesdrop unnoticed and to listen closely to seemingly irrelevant and disconnected bits of conversation, and piece them together, I know a great deal about that farm and how my Grandfather came into it.

It once belonged to my Grandmother's father, a white man, "Old Mr. Hudson." It was also once a breeding farm, a part of the unspoken history of America, a history that was more real, and more important than George Washington's wooden teeth, or his chopping down a cherry tree and lying about never telling a lie.

During the antebellum period of American Slavery, a perfect storm occurred.

First, in 1793, an enterprising young man by the name of Eli Whitney invented the Cotton Gin. The mechanization of spinning in England had created a greatly expanded market for U.S. cotton, but production was bottlenecked by the manual removal of the seeds from the raw fiber. The Cotton Gin changed that, and is credited with making cotton virtually the only crop of the U.S. south. It became the oil of its day.

Second, the United States doubled in size in 1803 with Thomas Jefferson's Louisiana Purchase, as Deep South states like Alabama, Mississippi, Louisiana, became a part of the young country.

Third, there was Mother Nature, or the nature of the climate. Here's what I wrote in an essay in my book, *The Rejected American*, after attending a NAACP Convention in Nashville, Tennessee, in the middle of July: "As I stepped off the plane on that late July day and the heavy, oppressive southern air hit me, I immediately understood slavery once again, as I had a few years earlier on a late July day in New Orleans, or a few years before that in Baltimore, Dallas and Washington, D.C.

"Before machines, and fans, and air conditioning, this rich land was useless to the Northern Europeans. How could they have made use of this land without the African?"

Here's how Governor Johnson of Georgia, in a speech in Philadelphia on Sept. 17, 1856, bluntly put the problem the whites faced, thinking as I had, years later: "They cannot hire labor to cultivate rice swamps, ditch their low ground, or drain their morasses. And why? Because the climate is deadly to the white man. He could not go there and live a week; and therefore the vast territory would be a barren waste unless Capital owned labor."

All of this created a greater demand for slaves. This demand was compounded by the fact that the African slave trade officially ended in

1810. So when we get to the antebellum period of American slavery, any high-minded talk of possible freedom for blacks slowly came to an end in the south. As David Brion Davis notes in his thoughtful little book, *Challenging the Boundaries of Slavery,* "Southern slave-grown cotton was by far the nation's leading export. It powered textile manufacturing in both New England and England, and it paid for American imports of everything from steel to investment capital. Moreover, since the price of slaves continued to soar through the antebellum decades, American slaves represented more capital than any other asset in the nation, with the exception of land. In 1860, the value of Southern slaves was about three times the value of the capital stock in manufacturing and railroads nationwide."

This "black gold" ushered in one of the most horrendous aspects of American slavery: The Inter-state slave trade.

Breeding blacks for sale to the large cotton plantations in the Deep South, was far more profitable for my white relatives than growing crops. In this part of the world, from the end of the official slave trade in 1810, to the Civil War, the only crop that mattered was the one that would ultimately walk, talk, think, dream, and pick cotton.

***

But I knew nothing of this at such a young age, although this was a profound history I was personally and intimately connected to. In the year or so that I lived on my grandparents' farm, slavery was never spoken of, although everyone of us on that farm deep in rural North Virginia lived in the shadow of all the great themes in American history -- slavery, miscegenation, night riders, the bloody Civil War in which 600,000 combatants, 7 percent of the American population, died -- parts of which were fought on this very soil.

When I was staying there, someone was always uncovering something half buried in the soil: a confederate soldier's canteen here, a Union cap there, a spent musket shot, an Army issue belt buckle; all of which spoke in a quiet eloquence, of days not that long ago, days that were filled with the terrifying cries of the dying and injured, with dense smoke, awesome explosions, and bloody human limbs flying gruesomely through the air, torn suddenly apart from their bodies.

The air was also filled with tearful, fearful cries to an indifferent god, to "save me, please God, save me!"

This God the soldiers prayed so passionately to, so desperately to, did nothing to stop the brutality, but turned away, seemingly unconcerned; perhaps in a state of total disgust.

Or, perhaps, with a little tear, feeling a deep sympathy, or maybe feeling nothing -- allowed the carnage to go on, perhaps saying to itself, "This is what you deserve."

The unspeakable horrors this beautiful land once held – all because my English relatives didn't like picking cotton, but lusted after material things, and power over others, was now peaceful, with only those small reminders we kids found exploring our environment.

I only caught occasional whispers which hinted at this awful past, catching occasional knowing, inside jokes, including a comment my grandmother once made because I was so scrawny looking, that in the "old days" they would have been taken me out in the woods and shot me.

My wise grandfather only slowly, but knowingly, nodded his head, and then made his famous pronouncement: "That boy is going to be a preacher one day. Mark my words."

I didn't know who "they" were who wanted to shoot me, but I knew I didn't want to be a preacher, although I now know I was being paid a great compliment. When my grandmother took us to the little church that sat alone on a large lot of land in the middle of nowhere, on Sundays, I could barely contain my laughter. It seemed that the preacher was acting in such a stupid fashion, screaming at the top of his voice, waving his hands and arms around frantically, causing women to jump up and faint where they were standing, with the preacher running back and forth like someone possessed by an evil devil, and the entire church in an uproar.

It seemed to me that the preacher was acting just plain silly, even as he yelled, "Jesus, precious Jesus!," and caused women to faint dead away.

I would furtively glance over to one of my brothers and we would start giggling as my grandmother watched the preacher intently, entranced, as were all of the adults.

I remember that the preacher had a long, bald head with a slight indentation in the middle of his head. The kids called him "Two heads." After the word got out that my Grandfather said I would someday be just like him, the kids started teasing me unmercifully, and I was saddled with my first nickname, "Two heads."

Even at that young age, I knew with absolute certainty that I surely didn't want to be like that preacher, and I certainly didn't have two heads!

In the end, for me and my brothers, this large farm, with its many cousins and uncles and aunts, and who knows what else, was the playground of playgrounds. This was now our world. And what a world it was. It was filled with apple trees, peach trees, pear trees, bright red tomatoes, melons, corn, pigs, chickens, cows, two white horses, one a large male, the other a smaller female, who pulled the wagon that served as our means of transportation.

It was a world of "Slopping the hogs," canning fruits and vegetables, smoking hams; chopping wood for heat and cooking; milking the cow and making buttermilk and butter; getting water from the well for cooking, drinking and heating, taking a weekly bath in a large tin pot; chopping the head off a chicken for dinner, and watching and wondering how long it would run around, headless, until it would finally topple over.

The sight of the headless chicken would always bring loud laughter and amazement as we watched in utter fascination as the hapless chicken ran around from here to there, just like a chicken with no head on!

We would watch as my grandfather and uncles slaughtered the fat pigs, cleaned out the smelly outhouse, and gathered hay in large piles during the Fall. Delicious food was served daily on platters at a large table were everyone sat down together to enjoy the great meals grandmother had spent most of her waking time constantly preparing.

In many ways, I know now, with the exception of electricity, and a radio, this land, and this farm, which is still in my family, was exactly like it was in the "old days" when the European settlers owned the place, and a big, broad-shouldered black man was assured of having as much sex as he could handle, and a skinny little runt like me would have been taken to the woods and shot.

***

I have several strong memories implanted in my mind of those days. One was the day my friendly grandfather grabbed me between his legs and gave me several hard wracks to my small behind. It seemed that I had wandered off from the task he had assigned me to: pulling some weeds from the potato patch.

I learned two important lessons that day. One, farming was a very serious business. Second, Granddad, friendly fellow that he was, was not one to be messed with, and if he told you to do something, you sure as hell better do it!

The other small task assigned to me and my brothers -- Robert, who was one year younger, and Richard, who was four years older -- was to take the horses back to their pasture after they were unhitched from the wagon upon delivering grandfather, and whomever else, to the big house.

This evening, our cousin Junior, who was slightly older than Richard, joined us. He and I were riding the big male, and Richard and Robert were on the smaller female.

Soon, someone shouted, "Let's race!" and off we went, whooping and hollering at the top on our voices while slapping away at the horses.

The big male started pulling away, as I hung on tightly to Junior. All of a sudden the female stopped and bucked, throwing Richard to the ground, and I watched as Robert flew straight up into the air and landed hard on his head.

It seemed that Richard, seeing that he was going to lose the race, stabbed his horse with a pencil, which she took great exception to, almost killing Robert in the process. Robert turned out not to suffer any injury and neither did Richard. We later all laughed at what had happened.

After that, Richard acquired quite a reputation for doing wild and crazy things, as the story of how he stabbed the horse with a pencil spread amongst the children. But today, I think about how actor Christopher Reeve, Superman himself, was also thrown off a horse and landed on his head and died from it, and I shutter at what could have been the outcome for Robert. Instead, he survived to live a long, fruitful life.

The other memory is more vague, and still shrouded in deep mystery. On some occasions, I had to take some food to an elderly white couple who lived in a little run-down cabin deep in the mountainous woods. I think it stayed in my mind because their home sat next to a large nut tree. I can still remember gathering some nuts lying on the ground on my way back home. But who were these people? Why was grandmother so concerned about their survival, as she obviously was, as she told me more than once to hurry on with my package and not "dilly dally," and come right back?

I think I once heard someone say that they were related to "old Mr. Hudson," and were my grandmother's uncle and aunt, my great uncle, and great aunt.

Again, in those days there were just things no one spoke of, so who knows.

I never said anything to the old white couple, but just handed the old lady her food, and I think she would always smile, toothless, and ask, "How's Lula?" Lula was my grandmother.

***

Just like in Asbury Park, one day, without warning, a woman who looked like a younger version of my grandmother, and called herself our mother, showed up, and the next thing we knew, all four of us were on a train again, this time, we would soon learn, as the train slowly pulled out of Culpepper, Virginia, we were headed to Buffalo, New York.

I never saw my grandfather again. He died of colon cancer a few years after we had left, much, much too young, and the farm went into decline, as most of his twelve children, like blacks all across the south, fled north as soon as they could, to places like Detroit, Philadelphia, Buffalo, and in my mother's case, ultimately, New York City, desperately seeking to escape forever, the non-stop, back-breaking, primitive existence of the rural south.

My grandmother, however, lived on the farm well into until her nineties and it was my destiny as a teenager, to spend several more happy summers staying in that big, white house.

I am convinced that I took something important, something life sustaining from that brief stay with both of my grandparents at that young age. They had had 12 children, all of whom lived to adulthood. They had built one of the most thriving farms in Northern Virginia, and one of the largest one owned by blacks in the south, at a time in American history when hostilities against blacks were at their peak and most blacks lived in abject poverty.

Even as young as I was, I could see the great respect accorded my family, and especially to my grandfather, by everyone, black and white. I knew instinctively, in the very marrow of my being, that the Morton's were aristocrats, as far as aristocrats went in that part of the world. And I know now, without thinking about it, or saying it out loud, but just knowing silently that I had sprung from these two exceptional people-- that their influence has seen me through the many insults and perils that laid in wait for me as an adult in America.

And when Robert and I founded Morton Books, there was no question whose name it would bear.

Chapter Two, Time on the Cross

I remember vividly the first night in the place we would call "home" for almost the next seven years. Our mother had dropped us off at a large house in a black, middle-class section of Buffalo, New York, called Cold Springs. That first night I lay in a strange new bed with my brothers, Richard and Robert. I started crying loudly, "I wantta go home. I wantta go home."

Finally Richard said to me in a soft, sympathetic voice, "You are home."

I remember stopping my crying and thinking about what he had just said, and immediately saw the logic of his words. I did not shed a single tear after that and promptly fell asleep.

At this point, I should say a few words about my mother. She had always been tight-lipped about her past, but I have been able to put together a narrative of sorts; one, to be sure, that may only be a figment of my imagination but that could explain how we had ended up at this "home".

It seemed that when she was sixteen or so, some young, charming sharpie knocked her up. And it is easy to see why, because every male within a hundred miles of the farm must have had their eyes out for her, as she was extremely beautiful, a genuine beauty.

Still, in those days this was considered a major disgrace to the family, especially a prominent, proud family like the Morton's, and either a hasty shotgun marriage was arranged, or, if the would-be beau was totally unacceptable, he ran for his life, and the girl was quietly sent away to a distant relative to have her baby.

In my mother's case, she was sent to an older sister who was living in Asbury Park, then a lively resort city in New Jersey that offered a lot of work for poor, uneducated blacks from the south. That's where Richard was born, and that's where she met my father.

I know nothing about my father, just as Richard knew nothing about his. I don't remember living with either my mother or my father.. I have a vague memory of my father taking me to a parade, and later, a crowded bar with a loud jukebox. However, I am not sure that that actually indeed did happen.

***

So there we were, in yet another home in Buffalo, New York. This "home," which was to be our only home for the next seven years, was run by a heavy-set, dark-skinned woman by the name of Mrs. Thompson. She took kids in, who came from a variety of sources. At times, there was up to sixteen, or as few as four. Kids came and went (some deeply disturbed), but we stayed, year after year.

I have written about Mrs. Thompson in both essays and fiction. This woman, more than anyone else I have met in my life, has haunted my memories. Perhaps it was because it my first confrontation with pure evil. Here is how I had my character, the urbane, brilliant Art historian, Dr. Lawrence Ridley, in my novel, *Orphans,* describe her to his friend, a fellow orphan, the lovely Iris:

Professor Ridley continued speaking about the "home" that he knew. He was a thin, light brown-skinned man with a well trimmed little beard and small round glasses. He looked to be in his mid-forties, but he had just told Iris that he had just turned 50.

"The big five O." he had said to her, widening his eyes in mock horror. Scorpio. And you?"

"Cancer."

Iris didn't bother to volunteer the information that she was five years older than him. He also looked exactly like what she would expect a college professor to look like.

"Terror, as you well know," he continued, as he returned to the story of his younger life, "is random, unexpected violence;, the headlines in the newspapers and on television have taught us all that." he said. "But our terror had nothing to do with religion, or territory, or oil; it was just about someone who wanted to control us poor wretched little orphans, for reasons I can only guess. We'd be sitting at the dinner table and she would just reach out and pop one of us hard upside the head. The poor victim would slowly pick him or her self off the floor and ask: 'What did I do? What was that for?'

"Mrs. Thompson would just keep eating her fried chicken indifferently, not even bothering to look at the deeply hurt child."

"You didn't do anything," she would say, finally. "That was just in case you might be thinking of doing something."

"Oh my god!," Iris said, her brown eyes opening wide in horror. She could feel the pain even more because she knew what being in a home meant; poor children trapped, with nowhere to go, and no one to tell their stories of woe to.

This wasn't the early 50s, when married woman didn't have first names, and men and women both wore hats. It was the late 50s and the early 60s, when few people cared about orphans, especially black ones.

"Her favorite little trick was to hide behind the door with her famous ironing cord, and light into us as we walked in the door," Professor Ridley continued.

"WHACK! WHACK! WHACK! I can still feel the pain of that ironing cord and the confused panic as I tried to escape her. Jesus! How could anyone want to torment little children like that? I mean what did she get out of it? I still don't understand it."

Professor Ridley looked at Iris as if he wanted her to give him some answers to something that he had thought about most of his life.

He continued on, not waiting for an answer to his question. "But I personally escaped most of her wrath. For some reason, I had that old fat bitch wrapped around my little fingers. I became her willing slave. But in many ways, she became my willing slave. I would smile at her, flatter her, tell her how beautiful she was when she was going out, with her old-fashioned string of fox fur, each fox in a death bite on the other, wrapped around her neck."

"You look so beautiful tonight, Mrs. Thompson," I would say.

"Her fat, dark-skinned face would light up, and I knew I had her in my tiny little grip. I ran all her errands, washed her large back when she took her weekly bath, rubbed down her big tits with the soapy water, and warmed her bed for her when she went out, so that when she came back home late at night on wintry nights full of the cold and snow, she could climb into a warm comfortable bed, and lay next to my little body.

"I was able to steal money from her purse, a dime here, a dime there, nothing too much; and as I think about it, she probably knew I was stealing

from her, but let me do so. I was able to buy food for myself and the other kids with that money, because we rarely had enough to eat.

"Yes, she used me, but I used her as well. I was the provider for the other kids, bringing them day-old donuts, which a nearby bakery sold by the bag for a dollar, and candy they wouldn't otherwise have gotten. I had figured out a way to help them. And I never told them how I did it. I just showed up with the food."

As horrified as she was by his story, which he delivered with slow, professional calm, Iris instantly got it. Yes, she thought to herself, he was a clever, lovely, highly intelligent little charmer just like she had been.

He had the same instincts, and intuitive understanding of human nature that she was gifted with, which her poor brother, Stephan, did not share. Stephan was wrong about one thing: it wasn't only women who had these skills. Professor Ridley was living proof of that.

***

As always, the fiction writer is never to be completely believed. His creations are often unreliable witnesses, not to be trusted, because they are people who never let truth get in the way of a good story, even though many people like to believe that most fiction is autobiographical (and most autobiography is really fiction!) But, after all, the very art and essence of the writer of fiction is the ability to tell a convincing lie.

In this case, the real story took place in the late 40s and early 50s, and the true hero in that home was not me, but my brother Richard. Yes, I took great pleasure in out-thinking and charming Mrs. Thompson, but it was a smart, deliberate, mental war. I worked quietly in the shadows; no one, not even my brothers, knew what I was up to.

Richard was openly defiant, saying in clear, unmistakable terms, "Fuck you bitch!" Her ironing cord didn't intimidate him, although he was on the receiving end more often than anyone else. Richard was the one who would steal out of the upper floor window, cross the roof, and bring us back the day old donuts, and whatever other food he could lay his hands on.

That's when I first discovered that it was a good thing to have a mean older brother that did wild and crazy things. I can see now that he was at once our father, mother and older brother, and that he took his role very seriously.

One day Mrs. Thompson told us that the woman who came to visit us once every few years was not really our mother, but a social worker. She would visit and sit quietly, but watchfully, in the living room with us and Mrs. Thompson. offering little.

I knew that low-life Mrs. Thompson was lying. But yet, there was still a small, nagging doubt. I wrote about these feelings in my novel, Orphans, as Professor Ridley's related his story to his friend, Iris, who also grew up in a home from the tender age of four, with her brother Stephan, then eight, for 15 years.

His story stayed fixed in her mind, and flooded it with her own private memories:

By the time my mother died I barely knew her. I was 19, working, and living on my own. She was living in a home herself, in a large state institution on Long Island, NY, Pilgrim State Hospital. She was there those many years due to depression, and although she forayed out into the world on several occasions, she never could make it on her own.

I remember what Professor Ridley said to me concerning his mother. It was so touching. He said he never knew her or his father. In that sense he was a truer orphan than I. He said he remembered walking the streets of Buffalo as a young child and staring into the faces of women whom he imagined to be his mother's age. He would look at them closely; even following them a few blocks just to get a better look, wondering if one of them was his mother. He hadn't seen her since he was two or three.

"I saw my mother once on those streets, or at least in my young mind, I convinced myself that the woman I saw that day was my mother," he told me.

"How could you tell? Did you know even what your mother looked like or that she even lived in the same town?" I asked.

"I think I heard she left for New York, or went back to her home in the south. Who knows? But I remembered that she was tall. Yes, tall, very tall and very beautiful. With soft, light brown skin and a kindly, intelligent face. That's the woman I saw cross the street.

"I started following her. I walked carefully behind her for several blocks, often losing sight of her because of the other people on the street. I darted in and out of the people on the crowded street with my little self, pushing slow moving, unconcerned strollers out of the way, and trying my best to keep up with the woman that I just knew was my mother.

"But soon the other people enveloped her, and she just disappeared, never once noticing me.

"I thought about that wonderful, beautiful woman for months, and even dreamed that she came to The Home and kissed me good night and promised me that she was going to come and take me away from the evil Mrs. Thompson.

"You promise me, momma?" I asked her, tears in my innocent young eyes.

"By now, I could see that she also had tears in her eyes. She pulled me to her and held me close to her breast."

"Yes son, my beloved, handsome gifted son," she said. "I'll come and get you. Don't you worry."

"She started to softly rub my head in a slow, loving manner, so full of love, kindness, and deep sympathy for my unfortunate plight. She started humming quietly to herself a lullaby and started rocking me back and forth. Soon, I was engulfed in a sound, peaceful sleep. I slept as only a young child would sleep if they were as sure as I, that they were loved and protected, and with the person who would never abandon them, but always love them unconditionally.

"Of course, she never came to rescue me. It was all in my mind, Iris. All in my mind, dear. Nevertheless, I came back to the same corner in Buffalo over and over again, but never again saw the woman who I spotted on the street that day, and who later came to me in my dreams; the woman who cried with me as she gently rubbed my head; the woman who I knew was my mother."

I felt like shedding a heartfelt tear as my friend Professor Ridley calmly told me this story. How many times have I heard variations of that story over the years at The Home.

Of course their parents were tall! For a little kid, everyone was tall. But being tall told little. Some of the kids who had no idea who or what their parents were really like would tell me stories about how their "tall" parents were members of the Royal family from whatever country their ancestors were from. Others belonged to The Mafia. Or their fathers were great ballplayers; their mothers, great beauties. They were rich and lived in *mansions and had colored servants. They were movie stars and friends of the President.*

What I saw most was longing on the faces of the kids telling these stories. Their young faces would take on a faraway, dreamy look, as they described their wonderful, make-believe parents. I never interrupted them and told them they were full of it, as some kids would.

***

Wonderful, insightful writing. For once, the unreliable novelist got the story right, without too many embellishments and half-truths, and his story was highly nuanced, and brilliantly observed.

Chapter Three—The Bronx

We arrived back to our hometown of Asbury Park, New Jersey late at night sometimes in either late summer or early fall. I am reasonable sure that this was the time of year, because the next morning, when we ventured out doors to investigate our new environment, and look around, to my great surprise the street was full of uprooted trees, some of which had toppled onto cars and houses. Debris was everywhere, and the air was still humid with the warm breath of the topical Gulf of Mexico.

It seemed that the day before we arrived, a major hurricane had blown through, leaving this part of New Jersey in shambles.

I was sorry I missed out on all the excitement.

Our mother left the next day, still a mysterious figure. From the brief time we were together you could have imagined the shyness on all of our parts. I can remember only glancing at her every now and then, not knowing what to say.

I could see that my mother seemed a pleasant enough person. She was the opposite of Mrs. Thompson in almost every way. She was fair skinned, reflecting her multi-racial background, thin, soft-spoken and very very beautiful. Most young kids think that their mother is beautiful, but in this case it was true. There was an elegance and sense of pedigree that I detected, and that only now, years and years later, I fully understand.

But Robert and I soon learned that she was also cool, distant and did not like to talk to us. The day we were to leave Buffalo, we were seated on the train facing our mother. We were going to Asbury Park, New Jersey, to stay with our Aunt Sally because we had to stay there until my mother found us a place to live in New York City.

Although Richard had been the one who had led to this unexpected family reunion he was still laying in a hospital somewhere in Upstate New York.

Now we sat on the train headed out of Buffalo and away from the hateful, evil Mrs. Thompson. My brother and I wanted to talk about what had happened to us all of those years.

We sat there silently, saying nothing. And then the train started moving. Simultaneously, Robert and I started talking, and pouring out our story. We were both afraid to say a word while the train was still in the station; as if we both thought that the evil hand of Mrs. Thompson could still reach into the car and snatch our little scared asses back into her mean, hateful bosom.

Now we related years of shared grief. My mother soon stopped us. She said it was our own fault if we had suffered, that we should have called her if something was wrong, and she had spent all of her life working in our behalf.

We did not have the chance to mention that whenever she would call, Mrs. Thompson would get on the other end of the line and listen in.

She once beat Richard because he had said the wrong thing. She also used to tell us on a regular basis that the woman who called us, and who came to see us once a year, and who sent Mrs. Thompson money each month for our care, was not really our mother, but a "social worker" from the city, and not to be trusted.

Or, whenever she would pay us that yearly visit we would all sit in the living room with the always watchful Mrs. Thomson present the entire time. Mrs. Thompson was always somewhere near. How were we suppose to tell her what was happening to us?

***

The train to freedom slowly gathered momentum and my bother and I fell silent again. Robert and I said nothing ever again to our mother about Mrs. Thompson. We did not want her to feel guilty over what had happened to her children. It was better to forget. This personal history did not happen the way I thought it had happened. Buffalo and Mrs. Thompson did not happen. That was my first real history lesson: the victims rarely write history

On the other hand, Aunt Sally, and her husband, Uncle Duke, was just what we needed. Aunt Sally listened with growing disgust and anger as Robert and I were finally able to poured out years of pent-up emotions, as we recounted our tales of woe, and what our life was like for us at Mrs. Thompson's Home.

Her big, round face was filled with deep sympathy

I later heard her talking with someone over the phone. "Damn Louise, that child is so goddamn selfish. Imagine letting something like that happen to her children, sweets things. They are the sweetest little things. By God, I'm going to tell her what I think of her, just you wait."

I don't know if my mother got an earful from her pissed-off older sister, or not. Aunt Sally was fair skinned and a fat version of my mother and grandmother. Her life in the north had been met with great success. She and her husband had income property in several areas of the city, and was considered well off.

For days, whenever she looked at me, I saw her face fill with warmth and love. She plied us with soda pop, candy and all the good food we could eat. For the first time in seven years, we didn't go to bed hungry, and we could roam the outdoors freely, as we once did on grandfather's farm.

In a few weeks, this pleasant stay came to an end, as once again, the quiet, beautiful woman who called herself our mother showed up, and took us away, this time to the Bronx.

***

Memories of that first day in New York City are forever sheared in my mind because of one dramatic image. One of my mother's friends met us at the train station in Manhattan and drove us up to the Bronx. We had to drive through Harlem.

I was absolutely astonished. I had never seen anything like it before, of since. My mouth must have been hanging open. The streets of Harlem were full with thousands and thousands of black people. They were everywhere. The sidewalks were so crowded that people were walking in the streets, and the driver had to blow his horn so the car could get through.

***

The neighborhood we settled in in the Bronx was not nearly as colorful as Harlem. It was at the very end of the north Bronx, near the Westchester county line. Then, it was still underdeveloped, almost suburban like, even without a fancy New York City name like, Hell's Kitchen, Brownsville, South Bronx, Harlem, The Village, Bed-Sty.

It was nameless.

It was also almost all white, mostly Italians, as I was soon to discover.

But life in those first years in the Bronx was quite pleasant, especially compared to the madness we had just left. Richard joined us, and soon after, Pauline, a younger sister, who I had heard vague rumors of, joined us as well in that tiny basement apartment on 220th and Carpenter Avenue.

My mother was still cool, quiet and distanced, but she was highly intelligent and had a well-organized mind. She single-handedly worked full-time, kept the apartment clean, always had something good to eat ready each evening, and made sure we had a clean change of cloths. She also brought us a small, black and white television.

She also allowed us to run the streets, where I soon met up with all the other kids in my age group. My best friend became an Irish kid who lived just across the street in a tenement building. His name was Dennis McCleary.

As far as race was concerned, I never thought of it, and it never came up, except in an off-hand sort of way, every now and then. For example, when the fathers joined us in the park on the weekends when we played baseball. Then my name became "Jackie," which I understood to mean Jackie Robinson, who was tearing up the big leagues with the Brooklyn Dodgers.

The only other incident that seemed to carry racial overtones was at P.S. 113 Junior High School. This redheaded girl was planning a birthday party. All the little girls were excited as they gathered in the back of our homeroom classroom for a little meeting. As soon as I walked in, they all fell silent. They all then started throwing me quick, nervous little glances.

I was to learn later that the heated discussion in the back of our homeroom classroom was about me, and should they invite me, the only black kid in the class, and only one of seven in the entire school, to the party. I didn't get invited, but it was my first real lesson of what happens in America when black males and white women meet at an suspected intersection; in this case, the intersection was race and little white girls having an innocent birthday party.

***

Life with my best friend Dennis, and the rest of the guys, when we were as far away from little white girls as we could get—was non-stop fun and adventure. The grand Bronx River Park was just a block away, and was filled with little hills that became our ski slopes during winter. We would follow the Bronx River were ever it led us. It soon led us to a tunnel that led under the highway to a little waterfall. The river also led is the other way, all the way into Westchester County, where on bicycles, we would gawk at the big houses.

This was an age just before Americans became seriously addicted to electronics and indoor climate control. The outdoors then was our plugged in screen. We knew intimately every inch of our environment and the urban territory we called ours.

I chuckle now, and note how much things have changed, when I see the occasional child riding a bike in a typical middle-class community. They are helmeted from head to toe and a parent is seen hovering somewhere in the background.

It seems that electronic addiction has made the outdoors a dangerous, lonely, scary place.

Or maybe back then the streets were always crowded with people, and we occasionally bumped into teachers, or someone's mom, or many of the shop keepers; and many, if not most of the houses had a front porch. So we kids knew that although we were running around the streets and parks unescorted by any adults, we still sensed there were always eyes on us.

Chapter Four—Black folks

One day, after about five years into my years in the Bronx, something life changing occurred. I was fourteen. That day, when I walked into my homeroom class, there was a black kid sitting there, the first one we had, besides me. There were five other black kids in my junior high school, but until now, none in my homeroom, or in my grade.

His name was James Johnson. I don't remember being shocked, or having any emotions at all at seeing him. He was just another new kid.

However, in a few weeks I was in a state of wonderment as even more black kids started arriving, and even a few kids we called "Spanish," who were really mixed race people from Puerto Rico. What was this? Where were all of these kids coming from all of a sudden?

My older brother Richard first discovered what was going on. I learned from him that a large, low-income public housing project, The Edenwald Houses, had recently opened some ways from where we lived, but close enough for the kids from the projects to attend my school.

Richard was soon in hog heaven. He didn't like whites the way Robert and I took to them. In fact, he didn't like them at all, and called then dismissively, "fay boys," "patty boys," and "jive-ass squares."

Now, I can see that all of those nights in snowy Buffalo, sneaking out of the back window at The Home, and hanging out in the streets, had given him an education about being black that both Robert and I lacked. At last, for him, there were now low-income, fatherless, dancing young black people just like him (although he took after our mother, in that he was far lighter in complexion then any of us). Edenwald Projects quickly became his home away from home, as he rarely came home to Carpenter Avenue anymore.

I noticed right away that these students were somehow different than the ones I had become use to. Like most public schools in New York, our junior high had a three-tier system. The top tier, with the special classes, was mainly Jewish, including two black kids. The middle tier included Italians and a few Irish, and the other three blacks, including me.

Then there was the lowest tier, for the "retardos," as we called them, for the slow learners and mentally retarded. No one wanted to end up there! I soon noticed, however, that many of the kids from the projects ended up in this lowest tier even though they didn't appear retarded to me.

Certainly James Johnson wasn't retarded. We became instant best friends. He was a bright, talkative guy who later introduced me to the world of reading books, while simultaneously introducing me to the exciting world of black people, a world of which I knew very little.

***

Edenwald Projects, at 225th and Laconica Avenue, was quite a walk from my house on 219th and Carpenter Avenue, a half-a-block away from the Bronx River Park, and the famous river that ran through it. But James had invited me over to his place after school for the first time, and I couldn't wait to visit him. When I arrived, after making the long walk, I noticed that the Edenwald Houses consisted of many large buildings, interspersed with three story smaller structures.

I thought the place was beautiful. It was well spaced with trees and greenery everywhere. James lived on the 12th floor in one of the high-rises, and it was the highest I had ever been in my life.

We decided on that first day of my visit, to go to the playground. As we walked in, we noticed a large commotion coming from the baseball field. We ran over and watched a group of young kids, around the same age as we were, surrounding a white man. The white man had his shirt off and was short and well built. I noticed a deep scar on his right side.

"He was a Marine. He got a big knife stuck in his gut during the war. See the deep hole on his side?" James excitedly informed me.

The ex-Marine was soon laid out on the ground, as one of the kids suddenly struck him from behind with a baseball bat. The kids then started kicking him, and cursing and calling him names. Some adults finally ran over and stopped the kids from potentially killing the unfortunate white man.

I was in a state of total awe and shock. James Johnson, or JJ, (as he asked me to call him), on the other hand, was taking all of this in stride, almost as if he was merely watching a movie, or something on television, or an event he had witnessed time and time again.

All I saw was a man almost being nearly beaten to death by a bunch of kids.

I had never witnessed this level of violence before. With my Italian friends, there was always an undercurrent of violence I could barely detect, lurking silently in the background. They seemed to posses knowledge of things that non-Italians like me should never know. I could catch little exchanges that suggested to me that there were people they knew that I was to be very afraid of: like those guys with big necks that sat in front of candy stores during the summer, and sold us fireworks during the Forth of July holidays.

But wise guys whacking each other, as those whispers suggested, was one thing, and was done out of sight. This was in broad daylight, with many people watching. This was a rude awakening to the world of the projects.

What caused the black kids to initiate such a savage beating on the white ex-Marine, I never discovered. The unfortunate man had no doubt bravely faced down America's armed enemies all over the globe, as his deep scar demonstrated, but never faced anything quite like this, in what he called home.

The kids that committed such a brutal act ultimately became my friends. Richard had laid down the law to both Robert, and me that we should stop hanging out with patty boys, but instead hang with the Negroes, as we were called back then, in the projects.

Robert promptly gave him the finger. He saw no need to abandon his friends and walk miles out of his way just to hang out with people he didn't know.

Richard didn't need to tell me more than once, however. Unlike Robert, I loved the projects immediately.

***

There were several contrasts between the whites in my neighborhood and the blacks in the projects. The first thing that I noticed was the music and the dancing. Almost every day after school, we would end up at someone's apartment, and the music would come on, and everyone danced. There was a slow dance at the time called "The Grind," which was really just dry humping to the music. But afternoon, after afternoon, was "grind em' up" time!

It was the first time in my life that I was ever so close to a girl, and I absolutely loved it. With my white friends, we talked about girls, but kept far away from them. I couldn't imagine them in an apartment, unaccompanied by adults, pushing young girls up against the wall, grinding to the music.

They hated dancing, and so did I, up to that point. I can still see us in the rec-room at P.S. 113, as the dance teacher tried to match us up with some little girl, then forcing us to make awkward movements around the floor.

UGGGH!

But I loved the 'grind em' ups.' This was the first time I had experienced music and dance as an integral part of just existing. At The Home in Buffalo there was no music, only a mean, sadistic bitch scaring the pants off of us. Here, it wasn't a big deal. It was just something that was done, and done for great enjoyment.

In many ways, this was much more exciting than the violence.

Still, sex and violence were the main undercurrents I felt in the projects beginning with the first day of seeing that poor ex-marine almost pummeled to death. Many of the mothers, like my mother, worked full time. Those mothers that didn't work sat around all day, often with one of the projects' "sweet men," and drank, talked, and played cards all day. There were only one or two fathers, and they only made an appearance now and then.

This was the biggest contrast between my new life, and my old one. Fathers was a big part, if not the most important part of the lives of my white friends. Their mothers were typically friendly and loving people, ever hovering quietly in the background. But Pop was always the main actor, especially among the Italians. With the Irish, Pop was often the drunk seen staggering home after work, like Dennis' father.

For the Italians, it was always: "If Pop catches us, we're going to get it good." Or, Pop said. Or, Pop did. Always back to good old Pop.

For James Johnson, and his two younger brothers and sister, Pop had stayed in the South Bronx where he owned a little record store. For most of the others, like me, and my half-brother Richard, we didn't know who, or where Pop was.

The end result was that as our mothers worked hard to put food on our plates, or flittered the days away in a drunken haze, we kids spent most of our time unstructured and unsupervised.

So, what do 13, 14 and 15-year-old teenagers do when there are no adults around? Well, for me and my new found friends, we smoked dope, had sex, drank wine, played cards, played loud music, danced non-stop, and fought with each other at a drop of a dirty look, or a misspoken word.

Like Richard, I had suddenly landed in hog heaven.

Now, I couldn't stay away from the projects, despite the long walk. My former best friend, the only Irish kid on our block, Dennis McCreary, looked sad and hurt as I quickly walked by him one day, as I was headed to an amazing world he could never enter.

He had been a great friend, but I had a new best friend; and this new world James Johnson presented to me had proven to be irresistible.

I spent so much time at James' apartment, that his mother, Mrs. Johnson, started considering me part of the family. I sensed that she also thought that I was having a good influence on her son, in that I didn't come from the projects, and seemingly did not have that mean edge most of the kids in the projects had.

Still, the mean, hard-edged kids accepted me as one of them from the very beginning. No one messed with me and that gave me what inner city black kids today would now call "street creds."

I discerned, however, without ever really acknowledging it, that the real street creds were what my older brother had in spades.

Again, "Rabbit," Richard's new name because of how swift of foot he was, quickly established himself in Edenwald Projects as someone fearless, unpredictable, fast with his hands, and who could, and would, do wild and crazy things. He could out-drink; out-fight and out-fuck everyone.

So, once again, I hid behind his long coattails, and stuck my tongue out at anyone I didn't like, knowing full well that to deal with me also meant that you had to face Richard. And Richard had made it clear to everyone, that to mess with me, meant they had to deal with him, and no one wanted to deal with someone as crazy as he projected himself.

For my new adventure in the Edenwald Projects, it was good to have a mean older brother that everyone was sacred shitless of.

***

Robert, on the other hand, held steadfast. He remained wary of the projects, and saw no reason to abandon his friends on Carpenter Avenue, just because they were white. (Looking back, I can see this is perhaps why he was the only one of us to graduate from high school, while Richard and I both had our sorry asses thrown unceremoniously out into the streets, as almost all the kids in the projects, soon as we reached sixteen.)

***

I now know one of the major reasons why I took to the projects so quickly was not just the smell of sex in the air, or how quickly violence could flare up, but because of the sense of camaraderie I felt with the black kids, far stronger than anything I felt with the white kids.

I had learned quickly to give a wider berth to the truly angry, and the truly mean, although I knew I had a 1,000-pound gorilla standing over my left shoulder.

What really drew me back, day after day, was that no matter when I arrived at the projects, there were always some kids standing around outside. There was always a friend somewhere. This was 1954, New York City. By then, as has been captured in many books and films like West

Side Story, the entire city was carved up by teenagers of all races and ethnic groups into street gangs.

Even today, I have a mental map of New York City divided by "Bishops," "Chaplains," and "Fort Greene Stompers," in Brooklyn; "Sportmen," "Seven Crowns," The Golden Guineas," "Fordham Baldies," and "Italian Berettas," in the Bronx; and "Enchanters," "Redwings" and "Hell's Angels" in Manhattan. Some of these gangs were multi-borough, and alliances shifted and turned, and it was often hard to tell who was at war with whom.

I joined the Edenwald Enchanters, which had three branches. The mother club was in Harlem on 113th street while the other branch, which was mostly Puerto Rican, was in Alphabet City in the East Village.

Each branch was divided into seniors, juniors, tots and debs. Richard was obviously a senior. They were the guys who really ran things. I was a junior. Tots were pre-teen, but we had none of those. The debs were the girls, whose main duty was to carry the weapons the few times we went on a real "rumble."

We considered ourselves the baddest of the bad, while other gangs were just a bunch of jive-ass chumps and sissies. (Well, perhaps the mighty Chaplains in Brooklyn, and the white Redwings in East Harlem deserved a little respect, but everyone else was not to be taken that seriously).

***

I was still very naive in this world of blacks. The first thing that James Johnson did was to teach me how to walk. White boys just walked, black guys bopped. There was a huge difference. I followed James' lead as we walked down White Plains Road, with me trying my best to bop away.

"No, no, you got to move your head up and down like this, and your body has to bend a little," he instructed me.

He artfully demonstrated the walk to me. I then tried it his way.

He smiled widely. "Yeah, that's it."

I can see now that we were doing a modified version of the famous, wildly funny scene between Richard Pryor and Gene Wider in the film Stir Crazy. But James did manage to teach me to bop walk, and I kept bop walking, until the US Army bopped it right out of me.

(As I wrote this, as a much older man, now in his 60's, I was sitting in the brand new Santa Monica Public Library at one of the computers, out of a bank of 50, glad to be sharing myself with the other silent, intense computer users.

I was writing my memoirs. Who knows what they were writing.

As I walked out of the fancy new building into the bright, warm Southern California sun, I suddenly remembered what I had just written. Strangely enough, I then wondered if I could still bop walk.

I threw quick, furtive glances all around, quickly looking up and down the quiet streets, and saw no one. I smiled quietly to myself, and tried several bop steps, never quite getting it right.

It was clear that I could no longer bop walk, but it was a pleasant memory, nevertheless, but ultimately a foolish attempt at trying to recapture something that had been so important to me, so many years ago.)

What I noticed as a result of this incident of bob walking, and many other similar incidences, was that the blacks in the projects were extremely race conscious, much more than the white kids I knew. Perhaps if they were WASP, with a longer American memory, like the black kids obviously possessed, it would have been different; but for them, being Italian, Jewish or Irish informed their inner essence, more than their white skin.

For the project blacks, it was race, and they worked hard at defining themselves as different from whites as they could, unlike the handful of blacks that I knew in my area. In fact, the two black kids who lived the nearest to me, two light-skinned brothers, who even wore modified "duckasses," were members of the Golden Guineas.

My new friends had very clear ideas about what was right and wrong for a black to say, do, or wear, and especially what music to listen too. They sent out a clear message to me, telling me who we were as a people, which was quite new to me.

***

This was also an exciting time for African American music. Each week brought something new, which topped that which came before it. Myself, and the young blacks in the projects couldn't wait to hear what was next. Doo Wop was clearly the most popular, but there was also this hot thing someone had labeled rhythm and blues. My new friends in the projects lived for this exciting new music, and now, so did I.

No more Eddie Fisher for me! Suddenly names like the Harptones, Ruth Brown, The Orioles, Big Joe Turner, Clyde MacPhatter and The Drifters became important, far more important than Eddie Fisher had ever been.

And most importantly, I had a chance to hold the young, pretty project girls-- who I thought were absolutely wonderful-- even tighter, as we slow danced to the great voices of the Doo Wop groups:

"Life is but a dream, OWWW WEEEEE."

Great stuff.

I also witnessed a profound, revolutionary change take place during this period, which, ultimately, would soon help liberate America. But before I go into that, I will let the highly esteemed, former Associate Professor, Fred Beauford, the Media Historian, who has taught the subject at UC-Berkeley, the University of Southern California (USC), Cal State Northridge, and SUNY Old Westbury, take over this discussion briefly, and set the stage:

By now television was the primary form of visual entertainment, surpassing movies. When television first started gaining audiences and improving its programming, many thought that this was going to be a great boon for black people, that they would be included, unlike the movies, which, by and large, either ignored them, or held them up to ridicule.

The Eastern European Jewish moguls that had boldly seized control of the fledgling motion picture industry from Thomas Edison's Trust in 1914 by moving it to California, and making real movies complete with storyline— proved to be just as dismissive of African Americans as the old, ham-fisted, artistically challenged WASPS.

This brand new thing called television started out promisingly enough. William Paley, of CBS in the late 40s bet his entire strategy against rival NBC, then the most popular network. He enticed the two white men who created the black characters of The Amos and Andy Show, *the highest rating show ever, to jump from NBC and sign up with his network, giving CBS the rights to the show, which would eventually feature real blacks.*

In fact, by 1952 all three networks had at least one all black show. However, starting with the 1953 season, all three networks removed all black shows, and blacks were not to appear on network television, except occasionally in sports, the news, or a guest spot on a variety show, until 1967, with the exception of the short-lived Nat King Cole Show.

But while African Americans were being summarily banished from television, and America, the next year, they were about to begin an amazing journey to not to just say we are here, but to take center stage in American life.

In 1954, a disk jockey from Cleveland by the name of Alan Freed brought what was known as race music, or rhythm and blues, to radio station WINS in New York City. He had renamed the music "rock and roll."

It was soon all the rage in New York; and a year later, this magical, contagious music would become the rage all over the country after the release, in 1955, of the movie The Blackboard Jungle, *which helped make Bill Haley and the Comets' "Rock Around the Clock," the first rock and roll record to become number one on the Billboard charts.*

***

Amen. Thank you Professor Beauford for your enlighten words. Lord knows we need them.

***

If we are to believe Professor Beauford, It seems as if the entire country was saying goodbye to poor, unfortunate Eddie Fisher! And African

Americans artists had just been given a far larger American spotlight then they had ever experienced.

***

The professor was quite right. I saw it unfold first hand. One afternoon, while I was walking by P.S. 113, I heard a noise coming from the large rec-room that opened onto the street, I looked in and couldn't believe what I was seeing.

Here were all these white kids, most of whom were my former friends, actually joyfully dancing to the exact same kind of music I was listening to in the projects. The stiff moves we once had to endure during dance class were now long gone.

They almost looked like my new friends in the projects.

At first, the powers that be tried to put a white face on this music by having stiffs like Pat Boone cover black artists (imagine someone like him trying to cover a crazed Little Richard, of all people!). But young whites would soon have none of that pap, and wanted the real thing now that it was available to them by simply turning the dial on their radio.

Television may have dictated that blacks didn't exist, but those young whites I watched shaking their little butts off that afternoon after school at P.S 113, said otherwise.

This rock and roll era, which shoved a righteous finger in the face to the Bill Paley's of the world, lasted until the early 60's, and was once again a time when and black and white kids all danced to the same music.

Chapter five: Mother

Hanging out in the projects and being a member of a street gang wasn't all about listening to exciting music and dancing. It could sometimes be downright dangerous, and deadly. Also, I discovered that although typical New York teenagers in 1955 suffered from an existential dilemma that even Sartre couldn't solve, blacks kids were filled with an additional rage that could surface at any moment.

I didn't understand then, but do now, that this black rage was due to more than the typical teenage angst that inflicted almost every teenager in New York City, except, perhaps, Jewish-Americans. From what I could see, they went to schocl, had special classes after school in their religion and history, and never hung out with the Italians and the Irish, and certainly not with the few blacks. They seemed totally focused, and unaffected by all the angst swirling around them.

***

Jewish kids notwithstanding, one evening in 1955, I was to find out first hand just how deadly this urban teenage discomfort could be

.

As I have all ready mentioned, these street gangs could have branches in multiple Boroughs, plus shifting alliance. And, interestingly enough, given how segregated present day New York is, they weren't necessarily all of one race, or one ethnic group.

I still remember that the guy with the biggest reputation in the mighty Brooklyn Chaplains was the only white member of that gang. I also knew two light skinned brothers who lived near me, who were members of the Italian Berettas. I remember them wearing the same black motorcycle jacket and jeans, their hair pulled back tightly in a modified "duckass," just like their Italian buddies.

Our branch of the Edenwald Enchanters was all black, with the exception of two Puerto Ricans and one white guy. One of the Puerto Ricans was a short, mean tempered guy from the South Bronx. We called him Superman.

One day Superman had proposed at a meeting that we form a "brother club" with his old gang from the South Bronx, The Navahos. We all agreed. The first day our new friends, The Navahos, came to visit their new brothers they were wearing their colors, which were black and gold.

Unfortunately for them, the Edenwald Project was blocks away from the subway stop at 225th Street and White Plains Road, so they had to walk through the territory patrolled by the infamous Golden Guineas, most of whom were old friends of mine.

It turned out that my old friends, the Golden Guineas, had exactly the same colors and designs on their club jackets as the Navahos. They soon spotted the Navahos heading to meet us at the projects and chased their Puerto Rican asses back to the train station, sending them back to the South Bronx, lucky to be alive.

When Superman heard what had happened to his old buddies and our new brothers, he was furious.

He demanded a meeting of the Enchanters, which was granted. He demanded that we immediately declare war on the Golden Guineas. A member of the Navahos was in attendance at that meeting and told us that his gang had already declared war. That meant that by our agreement as a brother club, we really had little choice. We had to go to war.

The night of the "rumble," we were all to meet at the corner of 225th Street and Laconia Avenue, right across from the projects. As I stood waiting for the others to gather, I noticed that although a great number of Navahos had showed up, very few Enchanters were there, perhaps only four of us. I knew many members did not like Superman because he was Puerto Rican, and many thought he had a short man's complex because he was always "selling wolf tickets," which was one day going to get him, or someone else, killed.

Also, I knew that nobody wanted to mess with the Italians, including me, and not only because some were still my friends. First, they surrounded the projects, and outnumbered us 10 to 1. Second, they were what can only be called more technologically advanced than us.

We fought with fists, sticks, garrison belts, switchblades and makeshift "zipguns," which could explode in your face, causing more harm to the shooter then to any intended victim. We also walked or rode the subways and buses.

They had real guns, and drove cars. We knew that, and wanted no part of them if we could avoid it. As far as Richard and the rest of the Enchanters were concerned, these short little dumb ass Puerto Ricans from the South Bronx had come up here and started more trouble than we needed.

So, it was only me, Billy Barnes, Slim and Superman from the Enchanters, that showed up that evening.

We soon set out looking to encounter some Golden Guineas. We walked for a few blocks headed toward the Eastchester Projects. We soon encountered two white boys riding bikes. One was very tall and looked older than the other kid, although I found out later that they were both 15 years old.

We quickly surrcunded them. Superman suddenly pulled out a gun. I was surprised and a sudden feeling of dread overcame me. I had no idea anyone was carrying anything other than a few knives. I also knew Superman's reputation.

I must say, that tall white kid had a lot of nerve. Here he was, surrounded by a bunch of blacks and Puerto Ricans, with a gun pointed at him and he was staring Superman down.

"Either shoot me or get that fucking gun out of my face," I heard him say.

Badass Superman just stood there, staring back at the tall guy. The tall kid's friend did not look as brave, in fact, he looked scared to death.

Suddenly Tarzan, or Frank Santana, as I now know him, grabbed the gun from Superman and fired one shot. I did not see Blankenship hit the ground. I did see a surprised, puzzled look on his face. We all ran. I went directly to my house near where the shooting took place and went straight to bed.

The rest of the Enchanters and Navahos, for reasons which defy logic, or common sense, went back to the corner of 225th Street and Laconia Avenue and stood around, colors blazing.

The police had an easy time rounding them up. Everyone who was there at that killing did time, with the exception of me, and tall, bony Slim, who also managed to avoid arrest. No one told the police that I had been present, or my life would have taken a far different path than it did.

This killing caused a sensation and was one of the shocking crimes of the 50s. Tarzan faced the chair, but his lawyer Mark Lane got him off with 25 years to life. He served the entire 25 years.

***

I was on my way to teaching my media history class, as an Associate Professor at SUNY, Old Westbury, on February 17, 1993, when I opened a copy of the Daily News and my personal history stared out of the pages. There was a large photo of a young seventeen-year-old Frank Santana, in a leather jacket and looking glumly at a semi-automatic, which he had just recently used to kill someone. It was accompanied by a full-page story by Juan Gonzalez, detailing the sensational William Blankenship murder in 1955.

I was standing right next to the young Santana, who I only knew then as Tarzan, when he pulled the trigger.

I also learned that it was the shooting of Blankenship, along with other conflicts between Puerto Ricans and Italian street gangs, that inspired Leonard Bernstein to write West Side Story, turning the shooting into a modern version of the Romeo and Juliet story, while leaving out the blacks.

For the young Santana, however, there was no lovely Maria singing to him from the fire escape; just 25 years of hard time in the state pen.

Mr. Bernstein and many others made millions telling Superman's history, Tarzan's history and my history. But was it history?

****

In only a few years, the conversation among the gang members started changing, as one by one, they began their introduction into the criminal justice system. Names like "Warwick," "Elmira" and "Rikers" became a part of our everyday conversation. Warwick was the upstate reform school for kids younger than sixteen. Elmira was an adult jail located in upstate New York, where the older ones went. And Rikers Island was the local New York City jail. As the arrests grew, I would listen to long conversations about who was the meanest judge to face. Everyone agreed that it was the much feared, "Lebowitz." This judge showed no mercy to the young black men who stood before him, and everyone knew that if they were unfortunate to draw him, it was goodbye for a long, long time.

It was many years later that I discovered that the infamous Lebowitz, whom everybody feared, was none other than Samuel Lebowitz, the lawyer who defended the Scottsboro Boys, in one of the most famous trials in American history. This younger Lebowitz, in 1931, volunteered to go to Alabama and take up the cause of the nine black teenagers accused of raping two young white girls in a boxcar which all of them had stored away on. This was at a time when the Northern European settlers in the south hated Jews as much as they hated blacks, and didn't mind murdering them, either.

Up until this time, Lebowitz had been known only for defending mobsters, but he worked diligently on behalf of the Scottsboro boys, taking the case all the way to the Supreme Court, unintimidated by the great dangers he faced.

But now, years later, looking down on my friends from the Projects, this new Lebowitz, who had become world famous by helping save a destitute group of young blacks, and was made a judge in New York City for his heroic effort, had little mercy left in his heart for anyone young and black.

***

Perhaps you have noticed by now that I have not included myself among those who had to face the wrath of a Lebowitz. To this day, I have never spent one day in jail. In fact, the only time I have ever been arrested was for an outstanding warrant for a jaywalking ticket, I received in Los Angeles . I spent a few hours in jail until a friend bailed me out.

How did I do it when everyone around me, including Richard, was getting arrested on a regular basis?

For one, my mother sent both Robert and I to stay with our Grandmother on the large farm buried deep in rural Northern Virginia the very next day school was out, and we did not return to New York until the day before school started again. This happened until I was sixteen. As to be expected, most of the mayhem in the Projects, including young girls getting knocked up, at least four or five kids getting arrested, and someone either getting killed, or almost getting killed, or killing someone -- occurred during the summer months, and I missed out on all the action. Why she didn't send Richard along with us I will never know, because as a result of his staying in the city during the summer, his rap sheet just grew and grew.

But there was something else that kept me out of jail. I have two major traits that have served me well over the years. For some reason, I have always had an unerring sense of when it was time to leave a situation. I would suddenly feel in my inner marrow that things were going to become progressively worse. Perhaps it is because of my life-long ability to step back and evaluate, as a good novelist does, almost as a "fly on the wall," as a friend in San Francisco once dismissively said of me, and react rationally to a difficult situation, not emotionally.

Again, this is a trait that has often, until this very day, caused blacks, Hispanics, Asians, as well as whites – to look accusingly at me with narrow, unforgiving eyes, for being a bogus black, someone with ice water for blood, and someone not to be completely trusted.

An example of this trait in full flower was the first time my friend James Johnson was sent to jail. He and some other kids had stolen a car. I remember the car just like it was yesterday. It was a bright yellow and black Mercury. They had parked the car on Laconia Avenue that night and everyone went home. James told me about the car when I arrived at his apartment the next day. We soon joined four others at the car and were planning on going on a joyride. Everyone piled in.

For reasons unknown, something in me said, "Don't get in that car." I begged off.

"Aw, you jive-ass motherfucker, always got to do something different," one of my friends, who obviously didn't care that much for me, yelled.

That is my other lifelong trait: I am unmoved by peer pressure. My good friend Herb Boyd, the great writer, just said to me just recently, "You don't seem to give a shit about what people think of you."

Boyd is right, and on this day this trait paid off. I dismissed the harsh comment, unmoved, even coming from one of my friends, and watched as they pulled away. As soon as they drove from the curb, another car pulled out right after them. I knew instantly that that was not a good sign. The next day I went over to James' apartment. His younger brother, the tall, gawky Willinsey, answered the door.

"Where's James?" I asked.

"He's in jail," he replied.

"No shit!"

It seems that the stolen car had been staked out, just waiting for us to come back to drive it. The car that I saw pull out after them was, of course, the police, and stopped them only a block away. Everyone went to jail.

Soon, this uncanny luck I had of staying one jump ahead of the law, was beginning to generate much teasing. "They are going to get your black ass sooner or later," became a constant refrain. I was reminded of this in a scene from the movie Goodfellas, when all the wise guys came running when Henry Hill was finally arrested for the first time.

"I see you lost your cherry," one of the mobsters gleefully yelled to him, as the police led him off to jail.

But I never lost my cherry, so to speak.

One night, soon after that incident with the car, I thought my luck had finally run out and my black ass had indeed, been finally beaten.

About twenty of us had been drinking our favorite drink, white port and lemon juice, under the "wine street." That was a large tree we hung out under, in a patch of woods in the front of the projects. Uptown Bronx at that time was still very underdeveloped, and patches of woods and empty lots abounded.

If I remember it correctly, what set us off was that someone started talking about what had just happened to Emmitt Till a year earlier in Mississippi. The Klansmen who had killed him had just been acquitted in a recent trial. The more we drank, the more we wanted to go out and bash some white boys' heads.

After getting as lit up as one quart of wine could do among so many eager mouths, we soon headed out toward the Eastchester project; interestingly enough, following the same route I had followed a year ago, which had led to the murder of a 15 year-old white boy. We arrived at the middle-income project without incident.

We quickly encountered several black kids sitting on a bench. My brother Richard promptly got into a fright with one of them and knocked the guy out with one punch.

We left the project pumped up, with the guys excitedly chattering away, saying among other things, "Man, did you see that shit! Can you believe it? .Man, did you see what Rabbit did? Bam, one punch and the nigger was out cold."

As I have said over and over in this memoir, my older brother was very capable of doing wild and crazy things.

And just like that night with the Puerto Ricans from the South Bronx, we soon ran into two young white boys riding bikes right outside of the Eastchester projects. We surrounded them, and Benwine, one of the seniors, who got his nickname because he drank copious amounts of white port and lemon juice -- and anything else with alcohol in it -- suddenly pulled out a knife.

For reasons unbeknownst to me, I said, "Leave them alone. They're just little kids."

It just didn't seem right to me that 20 of us were picking on two, scared kids. At least Richard had squared off with someone his own size and knocked his dumb black ass out with just one punch.

What was so brave about what Benwine was about to do?

Benwine gave me a dirty look, and said to Richard. "How come that little nigger of yours always got something to say?"

"Aw, come on, forget about it. Let them go," Richard said. Before we walked away, Benwine reached over and smacked one of the white kids hard upside his head.

"That's for Emmitt Till," he said.

I was furious. I thought Benwine was a fucking coward. What the fuck did he prove by what he had done, hitting that kid like that! I was deeply ashamed for all of us. On the way back to the projects, I was walking alone in the back of the group, disgraced and sulking. Up front, conditions became increasingly rowdier as someone -- I think hard-hitting, mean Lennie -- threw a garbage can through a basement apartment window.

"That's for Emmitt Till, motherfucker!" he yelled.

The guys ahead of me were breaking off car antennas, smashing windows, and thank god no white person was encountered on the street, or else they would have been dead meat. As we neared Edenwald, all at once I saw at least a dozen police cars come out of nowhere and surround the guys.

Because I was way in the back, alone in a deep funk, I was not caught in the trap. I dropped down exactly where I was, and hid in the grass and bushes. I was soon able to make my way home, undetected.

To my surprise, when I arrived home, Richard was already in bed, sound asleep. They didn't call him Rabbit for nothing.

In a few minutes, I was asleep, as well. But my peaceful sleep was soon interrupted as my mother came into the room and woke me.

"The police are here. They want to talk to you."

"Me? Why?"

"Just get dressed and come out and talk with them."

As I left the room, I heard Richard snicker. "They finally got your ass," he said, laughing.

The two policemen were ready to lead me out the door and down to the station house when I asked, "What did I do?"

One looked more closely at me. "Wait a minute, do you have an older brother?"

"Yeah."

"What's his name?"

"Richard."

"That's the one we want."

I went back into the bedroom. "They want you, not me." I climbed back in bed, and was soon fast asleep as Richard was led away to jail, and spent the next six months on Rikers, where he joined James Johnson and the other four guys from the stolen Mercury. It was Old Home's Week at

Rikers, as all of the older boys served at least four months, with Richard serving the longest time for that night of wine driven, politically charged mayhem.

Once again, I had escaped having to face an unforgiving Lebowitz, and once again, no one gave me up.

The one code we in the Edenwald Enchanters strictly adhered to, above all else, was that no one ratted on anyone; although someone -- a quiet, unknown enemy perhaps, who harbored great resentment at Richard's dominating, outsized personality, and the fact that all the young girls in the projects were crazy about him -- had clearly ratted on him, because the cops knew who they wanted, and where he lived.

But, as I now think about it, maybe that wasn't the case at all. Maybe it was just a watchful God giving me a thumbs up, and a reward to return to my quiet, peaceful, warm bed, unmolested, for having the courage to speak up, and save those two young white boys from Benwine's knife.

And if I hadn't spoke up, this God undoubtedly knew, being so wise, and able to peer far into the future, that Richard and Benwine, and perhaps myself, would probably have faced the same 25 to life that the young Santana faced.

***

At this point, I should say a bit more about my long suffering mother, as she tried to manage four children -- our half sister had recently joined us -- in gang-ridden New York City in the 50's, with at least two of us slightly crazed, testosterone charged knuckleheads, all by herself. My mother died in April, 2006, at the age of 87, as I was in the middle of writing this memoir. Her mother, my beloved grandmother, lived to be 92. (I hope that genetic gift of longevity has been passed on to me!)

As I have said, my mother didn't have that much to say to us, and was especially tightlipped about the job she faithfully went to, five days a week, and often on weekends, no matter what the weather was like outdoors.

There were obviously many questions in the back of my mind about her. Where did she live, and what did she do all those years we were apart? Why did she suddenly come and get us? Why did she then move us to an almost all white community?

How did she even find this place, so isolated, so underdeveloped, at the edge of the northwestern Bronx in the first place? Why did she always act so passive at all the shenanigans performed by Richard and me? I can never remember her yelling, or threatening us when we got into trouble, in all the years we lived together.

There was something far different about her than the mothers I met from the Edenwald Houses, or even the Italian mothers I knew. I had never seen even a vague hint of violence coming from her. I saw something vaguer, however, something which later, slowly, but ultimately, revealed itself fully to me.

I came to realize that my mother was a snob; that she really saw herself as an American aristocrat.

Many years later, thank God long before she died, and we became real friends, that I finally understood her.

The Jewish and Italian folks she encountered, no matter how much money they had, or the color of their skin, were in the end, still just immigrants, settlers, aliens, chased out of Europe by who knows what.

She wasn't afraid of them. And it wasn't her simply putting on false airs. I learned that her pride was something that she felt deeply, and that this was her self-image. Over the years, in my 50s, I discovered that as uneducated as she was, she still had a deep, intuitive understanding of the history of this country, and of the south, and her place in it; she fully understood the African and English blood (DNA) she carried, and it didn't conflict her.

Perhaps the most important thing she carried around with her, which she spoke of quite often -- adding that she alone was saving the place because she was the only one paying the taxes on the land-- was the fact that her father was once the largest black landowner in Northern Virginia, and that her grandfather was an Englishman, who had owned the property before my Grandfather acquired it, and all of that land is still in our family's hands, to this very day.

(An aside ... millions of acres of land were lost by African Americans in the South during this period, simple by them not paying the taxes on the property, sometimes only as little as $120,00 a year, which was what my mother faithfully sent the County each year.)

***

She obviously idolized her father, and I can see why few of the black men she had encountered in the north, and continued to encounter, given how attractive she remained until late in life -- never quite measured up to her standards.

This includes my father.

She reminded me every chance she got, that Grandfather was a "genius," and not so subtlety imply that she had inherited his great gift. She didn't have to convince me, however, that he was an extraordinary being. As you readers know, I had seen it first hand.

***

I am convinced that that was what gave my mother such a quiet, supreme, self-confidence.

(Another aside. I can hear a collective gasp and sudden recognition from those blacks and whites reading this, who know me well.:

"OMG. No wonder he's so damn weird. He takes after his mother, for God's sake!"

"He really thinks that he is a latter day American version of Louie the 14th, just because he has a French last name."

***

Not quite. But close.

***

I never once heard my mother complain about being an African American. To her, in many ways, it was a badge of honor. I realized later, that she felt at the very bottom of her being, that was made her a "real" American.

This was in startling contrast to Mrs. Thompson at The Home in Buffalo, as readers of this memoir well know.

***

I could not imagine my mother hitting me, no matter what craziness possessed me. Maybe she knew by the way I often snuck quick, hot teenage glances at her, that I saw her as an exceptionally attractive woman. I guess she knew that I had fallen in love with her, and that I couldn't quite believe that such a lovely person was really my mother.

***

She would only sigh in resignation at Richard's, or my, latest adventures. Robert, on the other hand, was a quiet, steadying force, and not prone to high drama.

Perhaps she was just overwhelmed by all of this sudden responsibility, and didn't know what to do, or say.

One of my best friends from the Projects, Buzzy, the guy with the beautiful, light green eyes and handsome, baby face, was committed to Warwick at the age of fourteen for doing half of what I was able to get away with. I can only now imagine what someone so good looking as Buzzy faced in jail at such a tender age, even though it was only a reform school.

When he told me that his mother was sending him away, I couldn't believe my ears. My mother would never think of doing something like that to Richard or me, although we probably deserved it more than Buzzy.

She just sighed, and sighed.

******

Slowly, I was able to piece together the fact that she worked for several wealthy Jewish families, as the help, as it were. One was the Chairman of 20th Century Fox. She had worked for them for years as a maid, cook and nanny. One family lived on Sutton Place in Manhattan; the other, the Freyberg's, lived in Westchester County.

The only real insight I got into her world was when she once told me, with a dreamy look on her face, that the apartment on Sutton Place was "the closest you could get to heaven without dying."

But it was the Freyberg's that always held my interest. One day my mother seemed very upset over something. She let it slip that one of the Freyberg's had just committed suicide. "I just don't understand why she did that, that poor woman," she said to me, in deep sadness. She obviously harbored strong feelings for that person because that woman's death obviously haunted her, and she kept coming back to it year after year.

She kept a small photo of the three Freyberg's children next to her bed. She had helped raise them from infancy. Although I didn't know them, and never met them, I hated them with a passion. I was jealous, plain and simple.

This was my lovely mother, no matter what they thought!

***

There were several lessons I learned from my mother as a teenager, when I wasn't out in the street acting like a fool. The first was that I learned to cook, and when you do cook, always have something green as part of a balanced meal to go along with the steaks, chops, rice, or potatoes. And don't drink stuff like Kool-Aid, but rather orange juice, water or some other fruit beverage. This was a far cry from the grim Dickinson plate of pinto beans, or plate of rice, or plate of potatoes that Mrs. Thompson placed before us nightly

My mother was the most organized person I have yet to meet. I would watch closely as my mother quickly whipped up the tasty, well-balanced meals she served us every night, all the time complaining about how hard she spent her life working for us.

This constant complaining would make me feel guilty, as if her personal misery was my fault. I developed this trait of feeling personally guilty for other peoples' suffering, as if I was some kind of failed God who hadn't delivered on my promise of universal happiness for all.

I wanted to say to my mother, "Let me cook. See, I know how."

I once gathered up the courage to ask her to let me fix dinner, but it was not to be. She quickly shooed me out of the kitchen, not giving me a chance to show off the tremendous cooking skills I knew now existed in my mind.

I understood what all that complaining was about, however. In essence, she was asking me for some kind of forgiveness for the years of neglect and mistreatment that Richard, Robert, and I had suffered at the hands of Mrs. Thompson.

Perhaps because of spending key developmental years in The Home, which I explored fully in my novel, Orphans, I now know I am unable to read people fully, and I am prone to believe that people are what they say, and not what they do, even at this late age, when I should know better.

I was greatly distressed that my mother worked hard all day and then had to come home to cook for us; because that's what she said, despite the great, loving care I saw her take with each and every meal.

One consequence of my wanting to learn to cook so that I could relieve the heavy burden placed on my mother was that I did turn out to be a good cook, just like her, and just by watching her at work.

I have been the cook for all of the women I have lived with over the years (my last girlfriend even had the nerve to accuse me of making her fat!).

My two youngest kids grew up in San Francisco, Los Angeles and New York City, with apartments and houses filled with wonderful, tantalizing aromas. And their friends would flock to our place, especially when they were greedy, ever hungry teenagers, because they all knew they could expect a good, home cooked meal, not a television dinner, or worse, MacDonald's.

(The last aside. As an adult, I still get very annoyed and non-understanding of people who can't cook. All it really takes is a little bit of this, a little bit of that, and overseeing, and watching over the preparation carefully, as you would a growing baby, until it all comes together. It's certainly not rocket science, and is one of the easiest things in the world to master; not to mention all the money you save and ill health you can avoid, by being able to quickly toss together a tasty, well-balanced meal!)

The other lesson my mother taught me was the concept of moderation. She firmly believed that you could do almost anything under the sun, if only you could learn to do it in moderation. Our meals were served in small portions, with room left over for dessert. She drank alcohol almost every night until her death, but I never once saw her drunk. To me, moderation, while often very difficult to live by, was a lesson to cherish.

Except for gout (perhaps because of too many, rich, well-cooked meals) I have so far escaped ill health and obesity, despite my drinking, smoking, and sometimes acting the fool with loose women. I am convinced that part of the reason is my ability to feed myself well, no matter what my income level, and to do whatever evil to my body I am prone to, in moderation.

Mother was right.

Chapter Seven—Death and Boredom

By the time I turned sixteen, the number of arrests of my friends in the Projects mounted; and now, the additional grim specter of death became a part of everyday gang conversation: LM died in jail, from what, we never knew, and George Morton was stabbed to death while walking down a street in the South Bronx. He locked eyes with a man sitting on his stoop, and soon words were exchanged. The man ran up to his apartment and came back down with a large butcher knife and plunged it into George's chest, killing him instantly. Around the same time, mean Billy Barnes threw musically talented Kush out of a seven-story window.

One death here, one arrest there, and soon the numbers started adding up, resulting in our group becoming increasingly smaller, and the Edenwald Enchanters became a mere shadow of its former, formidable self.

What I didn't know at the time was that something else laid in wait for my friends, and in about a short two and a half more years, an even deadlier plague, heroin, was going to descend upon the projects and sharply accelerate the mass extinction of this group of human beings, including my best friend, James Johnson.

In the eight years from my sixteenth birthday, out of the 33 members of the awesome Edenwald Enchanters, only five of us were still left alive (All of you budding Darwinists can make out of this what you will,; I have an interesting observation about the survivors. As I looked closely at who they were, it wasn't great intelligence that saved them. No one was brighter and more intellectual than James Johnson. As far as intelligence was concerned, in some perverse Darwinian logic, it was the highly intelligent and sensitive ones that first succumbed to the plague of drugs and senseless violence, almost as if high intelligence for young black males was a negative, dangerous trait to have; the skunk at the grand picnic that was America at that time.

It wasn't the color of their skin, either, in that the light-skinned ones, like "Big Red," and his brother "Crazy," one of my best friends, were most often the most angry, and most ready to give into violence. And it certainly wasn't the brave tough guys, like Lenny, another good friend of mine, who were quick with their hands, and who could knock you out with one punch. Nor was it the cold-blooded thugs like Billy Barnes and Superman, who carried knives and guns, and were prepared, without conscience, to use whatever force was needed to defend themselves, or take whatever they wanted.

Nor were the conflict avoiding, cowardly ones spared, or the sleek cats who swiftly ran up and down the basketball court in the playground, dazzling us with their high-flying skills, or the pretty boys like Roger Green, who paraded arounc, grandstanding on the corner, and showing off their incredible sense of style.

These considerable traits notwithstanding, in the end, they offered my friends in the projects little protection from this unknown, unseen power that was grimly determined to destroy them all, to eliminate this stream of humanity entirely from the human family.

No, the key trait that the survivors all shared, that was dismissively derided at the time, was being one of the "pussy-whipped, cock hounds," meaning, those guys who were always chasing after some girl, and preferred that activity to hanging with the guys.

Louie was a cock hound. As was Olay and Paul. They all survived.

In addition to being wild and crazy, and fleet of foot, my brother Richard was also a notorious cock hound.

He quickly found what he was looking for, however, and married his wife Jessie at an early age, giving up gangbanging. He borrowed my blue suit for his wedding, and I watched them get married at a Catholic Church in the South Bronx, where she was from. He stayed married to Jessie for thirty some years, and was never without a job after that. They had two sons, who both graduated from college.

Richard lived until his sixties. He died months after Jessie died of cancer. I believe it was of a broken heart.

***

The few times I visited him as a grown-up I would always see the sparkle come into his eyes as he relived the great days when he was sixteen, and was named Rabbit, the Prince, if not the King, of Edenwald Projects. ***

As for me, was I also one of the cock hounds? Well, I did write the infamous New York novel, *The Womanizer*, and I am still here, and even today I wander aimlessly the streets of New York City, like the gay poet Walt Whitman once did; and like him, I still feel that it is the sexiest place on earth, which, as Whitman once put it, "sex was just waiting around every corner;" and I can still feel stirring, and tiny tinglings in my old body as it remembers all the good times and beautiful young ladies that had come my way.

***

Let's just leave at that, or else I could be considered a sexual braggart, and who wants to be known as one of those. Besides, I now know what happens when you just "Let it all hang out." I got into enough trouble with *The Womanizer*, and who needs more of that.

***

School was a big blank. I had managed to graduate from junior high school, but I don't remember a single teacher, or anything I had learned. I do remember that my lifelong love affair for reading began in junior high school, when James Johnson would bring little paperback books to school.

He and I would sit in the back of the classroom with the books hidden in our laps behind large desks, reading away, while not paying any attention to anything the teacher was saying.

I clearly remember that the first book I read was 1984, by George Orwell. I had no idea then that it was considered a classic, and was read and studied by college students. James just said it was a good book, and it turned out that he was right.

When I wasn't reading, I almost always laid my head on my desk and fell asleep. Now, today, I still cannot believe that no one spotted the fact that I was reading at a college level, even in junior high school.

***

Sixteen was the legal age to be able to quit school, or be thrown out. I had barely finished one year of high school. School just wasn't for me. I found nothing of interest there. My teachers rewarded my indifference by indifference of their own. I left Evander Childs High School in the Bronx, in 1956. At that time it did not seem so strange, and was rather expected that a black male be asked to leave, or left on his own. In fact, most of us left on our own before being shown the door.

When I told my mother I was asked to leave, she did not seem in the least bit surprised. My brother Richard had already been tossed out a few years before.

And when I told my friends, they seemed almost relieved, as if to say, "It's about time, what took them so long," since almost all of them had long since been shown the door, or had left on their own.

In a quiet part of my mind, all of this deeply disappointed me. That quiet part screamed loudly, and longed for someone, anyone, to say, "No, don't do it. Stay in school. you can be just like the Freybergs." But no one, not family, friends, nor teachers, said anything like that.

I immediately went to work in the Garment Center, pushing "Jewish Cadillacs," as we called the heavy-laden carts that carried garments from place to place in the busy center. But I faced layoff after layoff, so most of the time I stood on the corner of 225th Street and Laconia Avenue.

This is when the fourth major trait that I have kicked in. Besides my calm, rational, almost detracted behavior under pressure, my ability to give the finger to peer group pressure, and my sense of guilt over things of which I have no control, is the fact that I get bored very easily.

I experience a terrible feeling of restlessness, and a profound longing for something interesting to do. At times, when I became really bored, I think I will almost burst with anxiety and would feel that I was slowly going crazy.

It has killed more relationships than I care to remember. My ex's would just look at me with sad eyes, and shake their heads and say, "You're just bored, aren't you?"

I would look away from them, unable to meet their eyes, full of guilt. Yes, I was bored, but it was nothing they had done to cause it. I just was just something I couldn't help, I really couldn't. How could I control a mind that was racing manically with unfulfilled desires and grand ideas, which caused me to pace back and forth, lay on the couch, jump up, lay back down and jump up again, while restlessness drove me slowly insane.

I always wanted to do something, go somewhere, and more than anything else, to have a conversation with someone who understood what was going on in my mind.

But who? And why?

I didn't know what to say to the women I loved, and the four children they bore me, about what was wrong with me; I just felt a deep sense of shame at making them so unhappy. The problem was compounded because I took after my mother in another way. As beautiful as she was, I was also very handsome, with brown eyes lighter than anyone I knew.

The young girls in the projects loved me. A musical standard from the 30s, "Them There Eyes," had a pop spin during that time: "I fell in love with you first time I looked into…" Well, you know the rest.

That song helped enormously. I could always find a girlfriend. (I can still remember running away from a group of girls from the projects that were chasing me because I didn't want to be bothered, for I just wanted to hang with the guys. Oh, for those good old days!

)

I knew that this feeling deep inside of me intimately caused me the greatest pain, because it produced many years of terrible loneliness that no one should face, as lovely woman after lovely woman just gave up on me.

***

I was immediately taken with the projects because life there seemed so exciting—filled with sex, danger and constant surprise, unlike the highly structured life I left behind on Carpenter Avenue. But as the years passed, and death, jail, booze, and dope took its deadly toll, I realized that this was not the same place it was in 1954, when I first arrived.

I soon grew bored out of my mind at standing on the corner staring out into space, closely watching everything that moved on the street. I was tried of the same conversations. I was tried of smoking dope and drinking wine all day, and walking back and forth from the playground to the corner, then back to the playground, and back to the corner. There had to be something else to life beside this, or a jail cell.

So, as soon as I turned eighteen, with the grateful blessing of my lovely mother, I joined a new street gang, this one armed with tanks, planes, missiles, ships, and "The Bomb," and left for the Army on March 15, 1958, and spent the next two years in Germany, with Elvis.

And that's where I became Fred Beauford.

Chapter Seven — Elvis

Before I formally begin this chapter, in the spirit of full disclosure, there is a very important, and highly interesting reason why I entitled this chapter "Elvis," when I could have just as easily entitled it "The Great, Life-changing I.Q. Test," or "Becoming Fred Beauford."

One day, during the 90's, while I was still an Associate Professor teaching my Media History class at SUNY/Old Westbury on Long Island, I was droning on and on in class. I looked up from my notes and noticed that many of my young students had that familiar faraway look on their youthful faces that clearly said: "When the fuck is this boring ass shit ever going to end!"

For some reason, I then mentioned that I had served for two years in the army with Elvis. To my knowledge, this was the first time I had ever shared this information with anyone. It just never seemed that important, and who the hell cared, anyway.

I didn't think that it was terribly important then, but for some reason it had just slipped out.

The impact of that statement was immediate. All of a sudden, all of those bored black, brown and white faces were fully awake, staring intently at me, clearly eager to hear more.

I was sure that it would have not had the same impact if I had told them that I walked with Martin Luther King Jr., broke bread with Gandhi, or once lectured Stalin on his evil ways.

Needless to say, I duly took note, and henceforth, managed to slip Elvis' name -- who semester after semester had now become "My friend, Elvis," "My main running buddy, Elvis," "My dear, dear best friend, good old Elvis" -- into lecture after lecture when discussing the history of Rock and Roll in this country.

I just hope that now, dear reader, this shameless bit of pandering and name-dropping will perk you up as well.

***

But before we get to Elvis, I arrived at Fort Dix, New Jersey on March 16, 1958, for army testing and processing. I thought of myself as being very clever at signing up in March, as I would avoid the heat of summer and the cold of winter while I endured basic training. I was sent to the barracks along with many other men; and when I say men, to me that's what they were, because the average age to be drafted back then was 24, and they were all draftees, with the possible exception of me. I had joined up just a few months into my eighteenth birthday, a mere kid and a fresh-faced teenager, compared to everyone else.

In a few weeks at Fort Dix, there was something else that I discovered, now that everyone called me Fred Beauford, not Fred Morton, a name I had known all of my life. I received this new name because the people at the enlistment office would not let me join without a birth certificate. When my mother finally showed me my birth certificate, the truth came out.

My name was Fred Beauford, not Fred Morton.

As I stood staring at the official document, my mother explained to me that she wanted all of her children to have the same last name, since four of us came from three different fathers, with Rob and I, full brothers.

***

I do not remember being taken that aback by this new discovery. In fact, I loved my new name. It had a nice ring to it. But first I had to learn how to pronounce the name everyone was now calling me. Was it BEEUford, or was it BOford? I had never heard anyone pronounce it before because it was a French name, swimming lonely in a sea of English or Spanish names.

Most people called me Beeuford, while a few others called me Boford, which is of course the correct French way to pronounce it.

I learned to respond to both, as I was unsure which was correct at the time. The issue was finally settled for good when I got to Germany, and a crusty old white-haired Staff Sergeant kept calling me Boford.

One of the young grunts had the nerve to correct him. "His name is Beeuford," he said to the Sergeant.

"Goddamit, you dumb ass fucking dickhead, I ain't blind. It says right there on his Goddamn jacket, Boford, you stupid shit-ass dickhead!"

Back then, it was not only okay for noncoms to call a recruit every insulting name they could think of, but they could also go hard upside his head if he still didn't quite get it.

From that day on, it was Boford.

***

For over a week at Fort Dix they gave us test after test. They were mostly about associations, using symbols and circles, and things like that. I had only had a year of high school before they threw my black ass in the streets, so I was glad these tests did not include math or English. It was called the army aptitude, or army I.Q. test.

I was later told that I scored 149. 149 sounded like an awfully low score to me, and I wasn't about to tell anyone that I was practically an idiot with a lowly I.Q. of only 149!

Little did I know then, that according to white society, with its classifications and so-called scientific measurements of human potential, I, the same person who was shown the door at Evander Childs High School after one year, and who didn't pass a single class the short time I was there -- was amongst the smarter people in the world.

The white boys test had said so, not me!

I soon noticed that the barracks around me were slowly emptying, as the new soldiers were given their assignments and sent to units around the country. Soon, I was the only one left in my large barrack.

I started becoming very lonely. "What's going on?" I asked one of the Sergeants.

"Don't worry about it, son. You should be getting your orders soon. They're just trying to find a place for you."

After a few more days of sleeping alone in an empty barrack with no one to talk to, that place they finally found for me was the Second Armored Division, at Fort Hood, Texas. After my first plane ride ever, we arrived at Fort Hood. I still remember a jack rabbit running across the runway as the plane made its landing.

The next morning the company commander addressed us.

"Tomorrow, I want you troops to know, Elvis Presley will be joining our company. I want ya'll to treat him just like any other soldier, and this includes the officers, noncoms and men. If I hear of anyone treating him in any other manner, they will answer to me. Am I understood?"

"Yes, sir!" we automatically roared in unison.

"I said, am I understood, ladies!"

"Yes, sir!!!!"

Needless to say, it didn't take long for that order to be ignored, first at Fort Hood, and later, in Germany. High-ranking officers all openly coveted Elvis' friendship, including the Air Force Captain who introduced him to his thirteen-year-old daughter, Priscilla.

I first saw him as he was unloading his duffel bag into his locker a few bunks down from me. I started staring at him. I couldn't help myself. He finally looked up and winked.

I was so embarrassed I lowered my head. If I had been white, I would have blushed a bright red.

Looking back, it is hard to imagine today a poor black teenager from the Bronx sharing the same Army barracks with say, Brad Pitt, or for that matter, any celebrity. The draft, which all American men from the ages of 18 to 35 faced in the 50's, was the great equalizer, and drew people together from all races, classes, and degrees of fame.

Just a year ago, I was watching this same cat three bunks down on television, and listening to my brother Richard yell, "Did you see that? That white boy actually moved!"

Elvis was indeed a sight to behold. He was acting like some white mutant. White boys didn't usually move much when they sang, but instead stood stiffly, like Eddie Fisher, only occasionally and awkwardly throwing out their arms. This guy moved around the stage so much, and with such skill, that the press nicknamed him, "Elvis the Pelvis."

As most of you know, when he appeared on the *Ed Sullivan Show*, he was shot from the waist up, for fear of shocking the nation with his wild gyrations.

But here he was, sleeping near enough to me that I could hear him snoring, and there I was.

***

Basic training, as anyone who has put on a uniform can attest to, is a hellish nightmare so most of us quickly got used to Elvis, and were simply worried about keeping loud, foul-mouthed Sergeants out of our face and getting enough sleep. But we couldn't help but notice that when we fell out in the morning, already in the distance, large crowds of girls had gathered. We could vaguely see them, but we could hear them shouting, "Elvis, Elvis!"

At the PX, when other soldiers from around the large base found out that he was in my outfit, I was offered cameras to take back with me to take his picture, and some offered to pay me if I got an autograph.

If I had had even the slightest bit of business savvy back then, I could have gotten over like a fat rat, as the saying goes.

Instead, I turned down the offers, feeling an interesting sense of privilege, because everyone on the huge base now knew that I slept with the great Elvis, so to speak, and they didn't.

I respected his privacy, and never even asked for an autograph for myself. However, I have often wondered, especially watching over the years America's unending love affair with him, just what an autographed picture of Elvis and me sitting together on his bunk would fetch today!

Elvis was not allowed to sing for us in the barracks. He explained that the contract he had with Colonel Tom Parker, his manager, forbid him from even humming in public or else he would forfeit his $600 dollar a week.

"$600 dollar a week!" someone said to him. "Shit, man, I'd stand on my fuckin' head for two years for that kind of money!"

We all cracked up, and even Elvis laughed, but I still couldn't conceive of anyone making $600 dollars a week, even Elvis.

On the troopship *SS Randall*, on the way to Germany, they put on a show. The crowd groaned, as we had previously heard in the barracks, it was once again explained to us that Elvis couldn't sing for us because of his contract with Col. Parker. Elvis did, however, sit down to the piano and played a mean boggie woogie.

In Germany, we were briefly assigned to the same company, but in a few months I was transferred to another tank unit as a driver.

The last time I saw Elvis I was on an alert, which sent my tank company, dashing somewhere in below freezing weather, me still in my blue suit as I had to run from a bar in town when the loud siren went off. I went to the motor pool, jumped in, hooked up my gear and started driving.

They loved pulling these alerts when the weather was below zero. I later learned it was because our huge, M-48 tanks wouldn't tear up the frozen ground.

My tank commander, a big Southern red-head second lieutenant, gave me a dirty look as I arrived at the motor pool, because I was in a dark blue suit and bright red tie and was obviously tanked up.

We drove for hours in the dead of night. I was just following the red lights in front of me. I was still half drunk and going where, I did not know, or even if this was a real war and the Soviets were really pouring thousands of tanks through the famous Pass which we were supposed to defend.

They told us in training classes that we were supposed to hold this Pass for at least a half a day.

"Then what?" someone once asked.

"We either stop them, get reinforced, get run over, or we nuke them!" the white training officer said confidently.

Back in 1959, I was too young to be scared, or even worried. I was just plain tired and wanted to go to sleep. Finally, I looked out and saw someone pulling road guard and directing me to make a left turn into a dim patch of woods. He looked cold and lonely out on this country road in the middle of nowhere, in below freezing weather somewhere near the border between East and West, and between Soviet Communism and the so-called democracy of America, which Elvis and I had both had pledged to die for, if needed, at the very height of the cold war.

That's Elvis! I'll be damned, I thought, recognizing my former friend's frozen, forlorn face, and suddenly coming fully awake for the first time that long cold night. What the fuck is he doing out here freezing his balls off?

I tried to wave to him, but knew he wouldn't have recognized me because it was the dead of night and my face was only partially exposed as I peered out from the underbelly of this huge machine, my head covered by a heavy helmet and communication gear. He must have already waved dozens of tanks into this patch of woods.

Elvis waved me on with furious arm motions.

The next day, as we continued our march, to where, I still did not know, I was tired and pissed off after getting only a few hours of sleep, with only the cold steel of my tank for a pillow, and was thinking about how Elvis could have avoided all of this bullshit that the rest of us had to go through.

But he, from the first day he showed up and winked at me, and was suddenly sleeping three bunks

down from me, asked for no special favors that I, or anyone else knew of, although they obviously existed, because he made Sergeant in only two years, which was unheard of in peacetime, and he ultimately married the Captain's daughter.

But as far as we were concerned, he was a "good ole boy," and did the same things that the rest of us did, and got down and dirty in the trenches like the rest of us, which made him very popular and genuinely well liked among the lowly grunts.

One final note about Elvis. In 2001, weeks after the attacks in New York City on the World Trade Center, I was teaching a History of the Mass Media course at Cal State Northridge. Of course, I name- dropped Elvis' name when I came to the History of Rock and Roll segment of my class. A young Hispanic man came up to me after class and explained that he was in the army reserves and he might be called up. He also informed me that that he had trained at Fort Hood.

"That building that you and Elvis stayed in is now preserved as a landmark," he said.

"Get out of here, you're kidding!"

That unexpected bit of information brought back another memory. One night while I was on guard duty, I passed by that same building and saw smoke coming out of it. I quickly ran inside and found that a drunken Sergeant had fallen asleep while smoking, and that his bed was on fire. I woke him up and together we quickly pulled the smoking mattress out to the street.

A few days later, the Sergeant that I had perhaps saved from injuries, came up to me and thanked me for what I had done. I soon saw a distinct change toward me by the noncoms. I can see now that that act served as forgiveness for being the biggest pain in the ass in basic training because of my defiant, mighty Edenwald Enchanters, smart-ass, bop-walking, know-it-all, in-your-face New York attitude, which greatly pissed off everyone, including some fellow recruits, and caused one young, baby-faced white Sergeant to take me aside one day and tell me to put up my dukes.

It seemed that I wasn't acting sufficiently angry enough during a baronet drill when I charged the dummy. The Sergeant had me run the drill over and over again in the blazing Texas sun.

Finally, when he told me to do it again, I said, "Fuck you!"

"What was that you said?

"Fuck you!"

"Come on, come on. I have something for you," he said, as he led me away from the rest of the troops and behind some large bushes.

"Okay, smart guy, put them up."

I willingly complied with his wishes, unintimidated. I put up my dukes as he had asked, ready to knock his country, white boy ass out.

He quickly socked me in the eye, knocking my dumb New York ass to the ground, and giving me a "blouse," as they called it in the macho world I was now in. He had "cleaned my clock" neatly with one punch, and that was the end of that fight!

The word quickly spread about what had happened. My new black eye didn't help dampen the rumors. The Company Commander later made the Sergeant apologize to me, because it was against the rules to beat up recruits, even if I was an idiot, wise-guy, black gang-banger from the Bronx.

***

But that was in the past, as I was now a hero. If I hadn't spotted that

smoke, that building may have been history instead of a landmark, along

with a quietly sleeping Elvis, and everyone else.

Chapter Eight — My Return to the Bronx

I didn't make much of a soldier. In fact, I hated being in the army. I think I broke some kind of record at my base in Germany as the longest ranking private in its history. It was only after I had three months to go that they finally gave me my first stripe. By that time, Elvis already had three.

In regards to race, I never saw that as much of a problem, even though for most of the time that I was in Germany, I was the only black in the Third platoon; and there was only one other black in the entire company except for two non-cons. Most blacks, I couldn't help but note at the time, were foot soldiers in the Infantry, not riding around in big, bad-ass tanks with gung-ho white boys.

I was used to being the only one, because, after all, until the Edenwald Projects were built in the upper Bronx, I knew only whites and I had little problem relating to them as people.

I was well-liked by the guys in my outfit, mainly, I think, because I was such an irrepressible little fast talking wiseass, acting both like a slick Italian and a street-wise black. I guess if you have already experienced seeing a person killed right in front of your face, and witnessed countless knifings and general violent mayhem like I had, that allowed one certain bragging rights.

I could hold my own in any conversation and I could tell that the guys didn't know quite what to make of me. One of the things I have discovered over the years, after living in various locations in the US, is that there is something about New Yorkers, whatever race or creed, that no matter where or what situation we find ourselves in with non-New Yorkers, we just think we have seen it all, done it all, known it all, and everyone else is simply a bunch of damn hicks or squares. It's buried deep in our DNA, and it's what makes us true New Yorkers.

True Californians, both north and south, especially hate us.

I was recently riding the slow, crowded No. 34 bus cross-town, when the white bus driver gave a woman some lip.

"I hate new Yorkers," she hissed, anger tensing her face.

Although I recognized the woman's frustration, given how slow bus service has become in New York City, and felt some empathy, I knew that the true New Yorkers on that bus wanted to give the bus driver a hi-five, and her the finger.

In the Army, I was exhibit # One for the ultimate obnoxious New Yorker. I was a stereotype come to full life, with this weird mixture of Italian, Jewish, African American and Irish background, which greatly amused the guys, all of whom, like Elvis, were in their mid to late twenties; draftees who hated the Army, and hated the fact that their lives had been so interrupted by all of this military bullshit.

This fact annoyed the holy shit out of the regular army non-cons, most of whom were WASP's, and blacks from the south. ""Niggers and hillbillies," I once overheard my friend from Maine say with a voice full of contempt when he thought I was asleep.

I still had my eyes closed as I heard another friend say softly to him, "Fred."

I imagined him putting a finger up to his lip.

The draftees, who were from all parts of the Untied States, and from all economic classes, cheered on anyone who had the nerve to give the finger to the army, as I did. I can see now why they got rid of the draft.

Also, I believe strongly that there was one other reason why I was so popular: I was cute, plain and simple. I was a slim, young, little "pretty boy" with a killer, baby-faced smile.

The U.S. Army then would be barely recognizable by those serving in it today. In my day, there were no women. There were a handful of German women who served as cooks in the mess hall, but that was it until you hit the local town and partied with the hookers. I once heard that there was a small group of women soldiers tucked away somewhere on our base, but I never saw any of them.

Rumor had it that they were all "homely dikes."

As one soldier put it to me, "Beauford, It's a good thing that you have never met one. Man, you don't know ugly! I wouldn't fuck one of them with *your* dick!"

We could go for months at a time, especially when on maneuvers, and not see or hear a woman's voice; so we cute little teenagers drew more attention than we often wanted. There were only three of us in our Company, and without saying so, we knew instinctively that some of those guys that were always in our face, saying what "great guys" we were, desired our company for more than our great personalities.

My friend Huff, the most handsome of the three, had so many "friends," that it gave a whole new meaning to the phrase, "watch your back."

Despite the crouch grabbing, macho, New York tough guy persona I tried hard to project, I was still very much aware of that fact that I was not without my share of admirers with more on their minds than just friendship.

***

But when all was said and done, the biggest problem I had in the army, and a problem that will plague me for the rest of my life, is that I have an almost pathological hatred of people giving me orders, and my not being able to have a say. In the army, as in most large organizations, it was yes sir this, and yes sir that! As the non-cons constantly explained to us, there was the right way, the wrong way, and the Army way.

On those rare occasions when I put myself on the couch, I see clearly a direct line from the time spent in The Home, to my sometimes strong, often irrational dislike of authority and people telling me what I should think and do.

I was that loudmouthed "little nigger who always had something to say," as Benwine had once so ungraciously characterized me back in the Bronx.

Needless to say, this didn't sit well with the army, and after two years we gladly parted company. But for many reasons, I am proud and glad that I served, managed to survive, and was given an honorable discharge. That time served has paid me back many times over, and is still paying, because as a vet I am not saddled with worries of healthcare costs like everyone else with little money.

As I say to my friends now, serving in the military can often be better than a college degree. When I graduated from N.Y.U., thanks in part to the new G.I. Bill that was enacted because of the Vietnam War, all they did was hand me a diploma and said, "bye."

The only downside to the military is that you have to listen to loud-mouthed, ignorant people yelling at you, and calling you names like "dickhead," and "stupid asshole;" and you just might get your head blown off, or have a 60 ton tank turn over on you, or lose a leg, an arm, or your life. But other than small things like that, it's a great experience, which pays dividends for life. In fact, in some cases, they will even bury you free of charge.

But at 20, all of the worrying about another scared young man in a different uniform blowing my head off was forever behind me. Once back home, I visited the projects a few times and did not like what I saw. The great plague, heroin, had it firmly in its grasp. Heroin had been introduced sometime in 1958, just after I left for the army.

James and his family had moved out of the projects and now lived on 222th Street in a house Mrs. Johnson had bought. The entire area had undergone great changes in the brief two years I was away.

This part of the Bronx was now undergoing rapid development. The empty lots that once served as short cuts for me were now filled with single-family attached houses. These new houses were different from the old, huge, three- story houses (like the one my mother finally bought on 216th Street and Bronxwood Avenue) that used to dominate this area.

Another big change was that the area was fast becoming all black. This was a time when the white flight to the suburbs was in full bloom. Although this part of the Bronx was as close to a suburb as you can get and still be living in New York City, my old white friends now wanted no part of it. In a few years it would be almost entirely black.

It wasn't just the Northwest Bronx that was undergoing dramatic changes. My first visit to Harlem in over two years revealed that it wasn't just the Edenwald Projects where death and destruction reigned supreme. Heroin had taken over Harlem with a fury. Everywhere there were nodding junkies. I even spotted guys I knew from the Enchanters standing on Lenox Avenue, lost in an inner world induced by that powerful drug.

Harlem was never a walk in the park, but now this place had become even more dangerous, as a growing army of $100 a day dope fiends prowled the Harlem streets, day and night, and stole anything that wasn't locked down, to feed their habit. They ripped off without conscience; their mothers, brothers, grandmothers—anyone and anybody.

How could businesses operate in such an environment? How could mothers raise children? How could little old ladies do the simple act of buying groceries, or going to church on Sundays and feel safe?

This white plague was to spell the beginning of the end of the once vibrant Harlem, as fear started to grip everyone; this was the same Harlem where, the first night I was in New York, there was so much bustling life that people had to walk in the streets. The great Harlem, home of brilliant poets, actors, dancers, and musical geniuses, was now dying and the rest of America just stood by and watched, doing nothing.

Uptown in the Bronx, it was just as bad. Neil was strung-out. So was Billy. And so, I was sad to learn, was my former best friend, James Johnson.

What happened to James was a true tragedy, in that he OD'd only a few weeks after he first tried the drug. I was with him the day before he died. We traveled down to the South Bronx together, where he was raised, and I tried not to notice how he kept nodding off as we rode the subway down to 165th Street. I didn't want to know that he was on drugs; if I ignored it, maybe it wasn't really happening.

But the next day, I was to learn that my head-in-the sand approach had failed badly. I knocked on his door and was quickly informed that he was dead.

Just like that, his young life was over.

A few years ago I had a letter to the editor published in *New York Magazine*. It was in reaction to a surprisingly well-researched article about how heroin once overtook Harlem. The writer got it exactly right.

"For a long time," I wrote, "I had trouble watching the movie, *The Godfather*. It wasn't until a few years ago that I sat and watched the entire movie on AMC. And yes, it was a great movie, a classic, in fact. I was even able to watch the part where the Italian gangsters were discussing this new, tremendously potential income stream from heroin.

"Only to the blacks," they agreed, siding with the great wisdom of The Godfather.

"That scene, and my intimate knowledge of what misery, death and destruction heroin led to when they flooded black communities with that deadly drug, had been what had kept me from watching that film all these years. In my mind, I couldn't understand how anyone could glorify such human beings. And glorify the Godfather, the film surely did.

"Sure, he loved opera, his family, and his cute little grandkids and was loyal to his circle of cronies, but he was a mass murderer and a destroyer of civilizations, and he did more to harm black people in this country than anyone in our short history. He murdered my best friend, James Johnson, the one who introduced me to the wonderful world of books. The Godfather destroyed the Edenwald Projects, and through the surge of heroin addiction, murdered so many more of my friends, and he murdered Harlem."

New York Magazine published most of my letter, but cut out the part where I compared what the Italian Gangsters did -- with a wink and a nod from the white establishment -- to the "small-pox laden blankets the English settlers once gave so generously to the unsuspecting Indians."

Chapter nine-- A slow awakening

Hanging out in the projects with the fellows was now history, and something I was totally uninterested in, even if there were no more fellows left to hang out with.

I now was free to pursue a woman who had asked me for my photo when I was home on leave. For most of the time in the army, I had fantasized that this lovely young person wanted my photo because she was madly in love with me.

Years later, I found myself rhapsodizing to her as to how faithful she had been, spending years waiting anxiously by the phone, pining away for my return from the service.

"That was really nice of you," I said, with love and gratitude dripping from my voice.

"What're you talking about? I was shocked when you called. I had forgotten all about you!"

Well, so much for fantasies. (I finally learned, after years and years of deep disappointment, to put to good use my strange habit of reading more into a situation with women than was actually there, by becoming a novelist. If I was always making things up in my mind, I may as well try to get paid for it!)

Nevertheless, persistence paid off, and she soon became my beautiful bride, and soon, my daughter Danielle was born. We lived in a low-income housing project in the South Bronx and I worked as a shipping clerk in a dead end job in the Garment Center in Manhattan.

This was my new life. The best I could hope for was a job in the post office, if I passed the test, which I heard was rough indeed.

But something mysterious started to happen to me. At first it was very subtle, but then it kept growing and growing and growing, like some strange cancer, destroying all inside of me that was old, and replacing it with something new, and strangely exhilarating.

It began simply enough. When I first was married, my lovely young wife and I lived in my old neighborhood in the upper Bronx. By now, the Italians where almost all gone, and the entire neighborhood that I grew up in (for years as the only black), was now almost completely black and Puerto Rican. It was amazing what had happened.

Riding the subway to 34th Street and Eighth Avenue, where the national clothing chain headquarters of Robert Hall's was located, was a little over an hour's ride on the crowded trains. Fortunately for me, because I lived near the end of the line (or the beginning), I always got a seat.

At first, I started going to sleep like most everyone else. I discovered, much to my discomfort, that by sleeping, when I arrived at 34th Street, I was more tired than when I first stepped foot on the train. To remedy this, I started buying a newspaper to keep up with sports.

I hadn't really read anything since school. There was no need to read. No one I knew read anything, so what good was it? Because of this, the reading at first was slow going. I had little understanding of most of the words. Soon, however, I started finishing the sports section halfway to my stop.

Now I was faced with a choice. Go back to sleep, stare out at nothing like most people were doing, or continue to read the newspaper. I bravely forged ahead. Now I was reading the entire newspaper before I arrived home that evening. Then I started finishing the entire paper before I arrived at 34th Street and would have to buy another newspaper for the long ride home.

This was the time just before the last major newspaper strike, and there were still a huge variety of newspapers to choose from: *The Daily News, The New York Post, The Journal-American, The Herald-Tribune, The Daily Mirror,* and *The New York Times*. I choose *The Daily News* for the morning ride, and *The Journal-American* for the evening trip back.

Back then I knew absolutely nothing about politics, or for that matter, much about anything. Right wing, left wing, the Cold War; they were names that meant nothing to me. No one I knew, including my lovely young wife, knew very much about anything, nor wanted to know much about anything. We were totally in the dark about what went on in the world, except what we saw, if we bothered to tune in, in the fifteen minutes of news that was broadcast each evening on television.

But all of this newspaper reading was slowly beginning to have an impact on me. First, I started noticing that when I had a discussion with almost anyone I knew, I always knew more then he or she about almost anything. It got to the point that my fellow workers at Robert Hall started jokingly calling me "Stein," my second Jewish nickname, short for Einstein.

In the projects, my first nickname was "Shultz," because everyone thought I was a cheapskate. I tried to tell them that Shultz was a German name, not necessarily Jewish, and they shouldn't talk about Jewish people like that, but it was to no avail.

Both of these nicknames, by two totally different groups of blacks, and years apart, had reached the same conclusion: that there was something strangely Jewish about me. I knew then of my English bloodline and my great-grandfather, "old Mr. Hudson," and my white family hidden deep in the hills of rural northern Virginia; but Jewish, which everyone swore I was, where did that come from?

At first I protested, because I knew from long experience how much blacks loved giving an unfortunate, select few, off-the-wall nicknames; and once they had fixed one on you, like "Two-heads," "Benwine," and "Rabbit," it was unchanging, permanent, and there was nothing you could do about it, whether you liked your new name, or not.

As an Enchanter, I once tried to nickname myself Robin, as in Batman and Robin, to little avail. Instead, I walked around the Edenwald projects for years being called "Shultz," until I left for the army.

But soon, at Robert Hall, I began to like being called Stein. Like my still new name, Beauford, it had nice a ring to it.

I started liking it a lot.

Now, many things started coming together. Like why out of 300 hundred soldiers at Fort Lee, when I entered, was I the only one sent to Fort Hood, Texas for Tank Training? They had given all of us an I.Q. test. I was later told that I scored only 149. I was so devastated by such a low score that I quickly put the I.Q. test out of my mind and thought little of it.

Then one day while reading one of those newspapers I now carried everywhere, I discovered that only a few people in the world, according to the people who ran the I.Q. test, were as smart as me!

149, especially the way the Army grades such tests, was off the charts. "Really!" I thought.

Maybe that is why, I thought at the time, that when I was in the Army all the blacks were in the infantry, while for almost two years, I found myself once again as the only black riding around in a big, mean ass tank with a bunch of gung-ho white boys!

I quickly dismissed that thought, but did start to notice one interesting thing. It suddenly became so clear: All of the people on the subway who looked like they were in charge of something were doing the same thing. All of the people who looked as if they were the low paid workers doing all of the hard work, were also doing the same thing.

One group was reading something--a newspaper, a book or a magazine. The other group was staring off into space, or sleeping. I leave it up to the reader to guess which group was doing what.

Slowly, ideas started to build in my mind. I began to see huge gaps in what I knew of the world. I was also beginning to be strongly influenced by these newspapers, in ways that surprised me. During the sixties, Chairman Khrushchev of the Soviet Union paid a visit to the U.N., and banged his shoe on the table.

Chairman Castro of Cuba was also in town, and deliberately thumbed his nose at America by moving his huge entourage from a fancy hotel in downtown Manhattan to the famous, but sagging Hotel Teresa in black Harlem.

I shopped often on 125th Street in Harlem and remember clearly the lines of pickets, both pro and anti-Castro. I had met a few exiles from Cuba because they started working at Robert Hall in the shipping department with me. I knew how strongly they felt about Castro, and what they felt was the destruction he was bringing to their beloved country.

What I remember most about them was not their politics, but the fact that they were all white, and the glasses they wore were large, black horn rimmed. The strange looking glasses I found odd. But what was even odder was the fact that I remember reading somewhere in one of my newspapers that Cuba was 75 per-cent black.

If that was so, where were the black exiles?

This particular day in Harlem, during the middle of all of this commotion, I was simply up there to buy a pair of shoes. When I was walking back to the subway, I passed the line of pickets shouting encouragement, or curses, at Castro and his cronies inside the hotel.

All of a sudden I became overwhelmed with anger. As I passed the group singing Castro's praises, I stopped and turned to face them.

"He's a goddamn Communist!" I hissed at them, filled with a raging contempt.

I had no explanation for my outburst. It is only now that I understand that part of it was because of the daily bombardment of anti-Castro rhetoric I was reading in the right wing newspaper, William R. Hearst's *The Journal-American*. This had fostered in me a deep, abiding fear and hatred of Castro, just as the editors of that paper wanted me to have, even if I really had no real understanding of just what Mr. Castro stood for.

But this was again the result of all of this reading.

***

Despite being sometimes politically manipulated, the end result over time was that I became more and more personally empowered; until one day, just like in a Hollywood movie, I woke up filled with an overwhelming feeling of self-confidence. It had taken over my body. I felt this enormous feeling of well-being, and physical and mental power.

I still do not know what happened to me. This is where the normal story of a wise mentor, priest, or teacher would come into play, but for me no such person existed. I could not point to one human being that caused what happened to me to happen. If I was religious, I would say that I was suddenly touched by the hand of God. Maybe I was? I have no way of proving if it happened, or if it did not happen that way.

Whatever happened, I astonished my working partner, Prince Lewis, that first day at work in my new life, with my new attitude.

"I got it man! I got it!" I said.

"You got what?" he said, a curious look on his dark face as I ran up to him that morning when we were about to start work.

I knew at the time that one of the collective bits of wisdom in the black community was that too much reading could make you soft in the head. Now, had I been driven crazy by all of that reading of white people's newspapers? I certainly must have sounded like that to my good friend Prince Lewis.

"The spirit! I got the spirit!" I said, because I didn't know quite what else to call this feeling that had now taken full procession of my body and mind so firmly.

Prince just laughed an easy laugh and we started work. But work was not the same anymore. Ii was no longer the worst drudgery on the face of the earth that had to be endured just to pay the rent, and put food on the table for my young family.

I was now above this simple, shit ass, racist place and could now endure anything Robert Hall threw at me. Who were these guys anyway but a bunch of creepy immigrants hiding behind the WASP name Robert Hall? Soon all of this would be behind me and they could keep their Garment Center!

That evening, my wife was to meet me at 225th Street and White Plains Road subway station after work. I ran down the steps to greet her.

I had been grinning crazily to myself the entire ride, still bursting with this strange, new kind of raw energy. I have read how cocaine addicts describe how good and energetic they feel when they take a hit. Well, some combination of chemicals must have been released into my blood stream, because now I felt powerful, and felt as if there was nothing I couldn't do, and I had felt that way all day. The feeling would just not leave me.

"I have the spirit!" I said to her, in exactly the same manner in which I had expressed my newfound self to my good friend Prince Lewis.

Suddenly my young, lovely wife did not look so glad to see me. And she replied exactly like Prince: "You got the what?"

Despite the barely concealed skepticism coming from my wife and my good friend, I knew I was now suffused with some kind of purpose in life; what, I still did not know. But I did know that I needed to fill the gaps in my education, and I wanted to learn about life now more than anything else in the world.

I started buying the books I read about in the newspapers. When I would finish reading one, I would look at the back of the book and then go out and buy the other books recommended.

My mind suddenly became very active; in fact, I was almost in a frenzy. I soon came up with the weird idea that I should one day run for President of the United States. Part of what was happening to me, I know now, was the tremendous impact that President John F. Kennedy was having on me.

For some reason, it always sounded like he was speaking directly to me when I watched him on television. When he was first elected, I was sorry that Richard Nixon had lost because *The Journal-American* had consistently pointed out during the heated campaign that Kennedy was up to no good, and the country needed the trustworthy, experienced hands of Nixon and his running mate, Henry Cabot Lodge.

Gullible as I was at the time, I believed them, and the first vote in my young life was for Richard Millhouse Nixon for President.

Still, Kennedy turned out not to be such a bad guy after all. Soon I started to like him. In fact, I liked him a lot. I now wanted to be just like him and as I did research into his background, I discovered that he had a law degree. If I were to aspire to becoming President, then I, too, would have to obtain a law degree. Next, I discovered that in order to get a law degree, you first had to have a college degree.

Oh Vey!

Hmmmmm.

All of this becoming President stuff was suddenly becoming very complicated. But first things first. I had to get a college degree, but I didn't even have a high school diploma.

I checked out some night schools and was told that I could attend part time and that in a few years I would obtain my high school diploma. A few years! I started calculating what those "few" years meant. I was 22 now. If I received a high school diploma by the age of 27, it would take another four years for a college degree, and another three to four years for a law degree.

I would be old as the hills by the time I finished. How the hell could I become President like that?!

A plan quickly came into my mind. I would take the exam I had heard about for a GED, or high school equivalency diploma. But how would I know what to study, since I did not know anyone who had attended college, or even had graduated from high school except my wife?

I started taking the trains near N.Y.U. and City College. I would look and see what books the students were reading, write them down in a little notebook, and then go into the campus bookstore and purchase the books and read them.

In a few months time, I was ready to take the exam and paid my fee, although I was warned by a few people who had taken the test that there was no way that I was going to be able to pass without proper tutoring, and I had not stepped a foot into an academic class room since 1956.

On the day of the big test, all of us hopefuls met at Washington Irvine High School in lower Manhattan. It was an extremely large room and there must have been at least 400 people there for the test. The test was given every six months, and as long as you were willing to pay the fee, you could take it as many times as you wanted.

In fact, the first question one of my fellow test takers asked me was how many times I had taken it.

He was a tall, thin, black man in his late twenties and one of the few blacks in the room. And he had a very serious, intelligent look about his face. I asked him how many times he had taken the test, and he replied seven. My heart sank somewhat.

"It's a hard test," he said, perhaps noticing the look of distress on my face.

It was a two-day ordeal. There were six different categories, including math and science. We all sat down at our desks. The person supervising the test sat at a raised desk above us, gave us instructions, and wished us good luck. And at last the test and the no. 2 pencils were passed out.

I picked up the test and quickly went over it, and suddenly started laughing out loud. "Are you guys kidding?"

The tall, thin, serious young black man who had befriended me and was sitting next to me, looked a bit startled by my behavior.

But I was on to something. This test was so easy I couldn't believe it! That is why I laughed so spontaneously. I quickly started answering the questions, and soon I was finished. I walked up to the man at the high desk and handed in my test.

"Do you want more paper?" he asked.

"No, I am finished," I said.

"Really?" he said, surprise in his voice and on his face. "Well, go wait in the hallway for the next test."

I first ran to the telephone and called my wife. "You won't believe how easy this is," I told her, excitedly.

I went back to Washington Irvine and waited for someone to join me in the hallway. It took an entire half hour for the next person to come out of the test room. The serious young black man did not come out for over an hour and was one of the last to finish his portion of the test.

I did not tell him how easy I found the test because I sensed that he was still having a hard time with it. And the other two tests that day went the same way, and the next day, the same.

In a few months I received in the mail the results and a new High School diploma. I looked at my test scores and was terribly disappointed. Just like my first reaction to my army test scores, these did not look like the test scores of a budding genius. But, nevertheless, I was now a high school graduate in less than six months from the day I decided to become President of the United States.

***

But this President thing was slow going. What next? My conditions did not improve at Robert Hall. One of the strongest arguments my friends made back in those days was that it was a pointless exercise for a black man to seek to improve himself, because no matter how smart he was, or how much education he had, the white man was never going to give him a break. This man was just inherently hateful, evil and fearful of others, so books were a waste of a black man's time.

This was the world before Affirmative Action, the good old days that conservatives love to muse over. Walk around mid-town Manhattan in 1963 and it was a white man's world. If there were blacks, they could be counted on to be carrying packages, or pushing brooms (has much changed, despite years of so-called Affirmative Action?).

Still, I relentlessly pushed myself to keep learning. I read of a college preparatory program given by the Department of Continuing Education at N.Y.U. but I could only afford one class. As I spoke with the person who advised me, he said that in order for me to formally enter college I would have to take at least seven more of these courses.

"There goes my Presidency," I thought. How was I going to do this? I was making $75.00 dollars a week. I had a wife and a kid, and was soon to learn that another one was on the way.

For the first time in my life I felt hopeless. Again, back in 1964, you were on your own. No one gave a shit if a young black man wanted to educate himself.

At the end of the college preparatory English class, I was wondering what to do next. I could no longer afford to take classes that were not leading to anything. I was ready for the real thing. I spotted in the back of the brochure that the department was offering a new degree program for adults. It was eight credits a semester and led to an Associate in Arts degree, and the classes sounded really interesting.

I decided to apply. I had no idea how I was going to pay for it, however.

I soon received a notice that I had to take the standard college entrance exam, which I did. I did not hear anything from N.Y.U. for weeks after that test, and soon forgot about it. Then one day a letter arrived in the mail. N.Y.U. wanted to meet with me.

I had to arrange my appointment on my lunch hour. I walked into the building at Washington Square and announced myself. The woman at the desk suddenly started smiling widely. She quickly walked into an office and out stepped this tall, smiling red headed white man.

"This is the guy. This is the guy," he kept repeating.

Everyone in the office, including the secretaries, were all smiling warmly at me. What the heck was going on?

"Come, come," he said, "I want you to meet the Dean."

I sat down with him and another white man, still wondering why everyone was smiling at me.

The red headed man noticed my puzzled look.

"You don't know what you did, do you?"

"I have no idea what you are talking about."

He opened my files. "Are you sure that you never took any classes after high school?"

"Just one," I said.

He shook his head in disbelief. Now he had my curiosity piqued.

"Look," he said, showing me a paper with some numbers on them. "Do you know that you scored in the top five percent of anyone in the country who ever took this college entrance exam? The top five percent! Most people send their kids to all kinds of expensive prep schools and they do not do nearly as well."

"Tell me about it," the Dean said, rolling his eyes.

"And," the big red headed man said, greatly enjoying telling this story and giving me all of this wonderful news, "do you know what you did on your GED exams?"

"No," I said, feeling the good feeling beginning to fade as I remembered those low looking scores.

"The top three percent!"

"Really?"

"Really."

Wow! This was too much. I could not believe my ears. Too bad there was not a camera around to record this meeting, as there is when blacks score big in sports. I had hit it out of the park. This was an intellectual home run. But the NAACP was never going to give me an award for what I had just done.

Still, this was the greatest moment of my life.

"You are just the guy we were hoping for when we started this program," the Dean added. "You are just the kind of person we want. In your letter you said that all you wanted was to do was learn. Well, we are here to teach you."

With that, he reached out his hand to mine, with the big red headed man still smiling warmly at me.

That is how I became a college student at N.Y.U. My mother gave me some money. I had saved a little money from my $75.00 a week job in the Garment Center, and the program gave me a little money. At that time I had no idea how I was going to remain and graduate, but in a little over a year after I came up with my crazy idea to become President of the United States, I not only had a high school diploma, but was a college student at one of the most prestigious universities in the country, long before open enrollment and Affirmative Action.

***

The program was excellent. I adjusted well to my new friends. To be quite frank, everyone fawned over me, because, in all due modesty, I was a pretty bright guy, and had many social skills, despite my poverty and lack of formal education. I was used to being around all types of people, whites included, and being the only person like me in a variety of social situations.

In 20/20 hindsight, I can see clearly that my wise mother picked an excellent location in The Upper Bronx for me to grow up as a true American. First, I walked around for years as an Italian, even going to Sunday Mass with my Italian friends, while they introduced me to pizza for the first time.

Next, I posed as a dangerous, black, teenage hood from the projects, and somehow avoided jail, drugs, or death.

My two years in the Army with my friend Elvis had also taught me many useful lessons. I had met people from all walks of life and from every part of the country.

And spending my formative years in a surrealistic, violent, unpredictable home for children, with year after year of watching kids come and go, and being unloved, and taught little, turned out to be a time well-spent (although I wouldn't want anyone else to experience the same thing. No child should have to go through that hell!), because that's where I first became accustomed to sudden change, and where I first learned how to think on my own.

And big change New York University certainly was. I knew that my fellow students and professors didn't quite know what to make of me; but I really sensed that they and the Dean felt good about themselves by having me in the program--especially a couple of the women who would fix their loving gazes on my smart, young black body in class.

Lucky for me, I was still "cute," but this time for smart, older Jewish women, not horny young soldiers, unsure of who they were.

I knew that those looks meant more than that they simply wanted to have a meaningful conversation with me.

Admiring white women notwithstanding, I soon began to grow impatient with the program. Not only because it was going to take four years, but then I still would be stuck with only an AA degree.

But the real reason for my discomfort was that I felt that somehow, the real action was during the day with the full time student.

I was an adult, but only a few years older than the average student. I was only 25, and of slim built. I watched those young students at the student center and started wanting to be with them, not with the old ladies I was stuck with in the evening. I was starting to feel like a second class citizen, although, as I was to later learn when I finally did transfer to full time--these well read, eager, middle aged women ran intellectual circles around their young daytime counterparts.

But a young man in heat rarely notices those kinds of things.

Chapter Ten—Social Action

The answers to my many problems would soon come my way. First, I was able to solve the problem of fees. At the outrageous cost of $75.00 per credit, NYU was among the most expensive schools in the country (we won't even talk about what it currently costs per credit, many year's later). I discovered that by working for the university, they would cover the cost for up to eight credits, just the amount that I was taking.

The day I walked into NYU's personnel office, I couldn't have been happier, because lo and behold, who should be sitting behind the desk interviewing me but a fellow by the name of John O'Neal. I had served with him in the Army.

John was a very unimposing, nondescript looking man, but he was memorable from my Army days because one afternoon, in the middle of the Atlantic Ocean, on a special entertainment program, he entertained the troops on our way to Germany on the SS Randall by playing the piano and singing "The Girl That I Marry."

As I have pointed out, Elvis was on the same program, and served as M.C. Elvis, graciously introduced John, calling his a great talent, in perhaps the highlight of his life.

Obviously, we troops were solely disappointed that we couldn't get the King himself and had to settle instead for a more subdued John O'Neal, who crooned in an old fashioned manner a not so bad version of "The Girl That I Marry." We were polite to John, however, and he carried his song off with aplomb.

Now there I was at NYU, sitting across from him, surprised and happy as all hell that he was sitting where he was. John quickly found me a job at a lab at the dental college cleaning up after the Graduate students, and that ended one of my monetary problems.

The second problem was my increasing restless energy. So much was going on. It was 1965. President Johnson had continued to escalate the war in Vietnam even after he was elected on a peace platform, and the protests in the streets were growing larger and angrier. The black movement in the south was also growing louder.

I was working during the day and sitting in class in the evening, totally uninvolved in this havoc that was swirling around me.

At first, I paid little attention to the war protest. I had just finished my Reserve time and the military could no longer touch me. Luckily for me I had the foresight to join at eighteen, because right about then the Draft Board would have come calling, and instead of me spending my evenings at NYU discussing Camus with a polite group of rich, intelligent, attractive, middle aged Jewish women, I surely would have ended up walking fearfully through steaming jungles and dank patty fields of rice in Southeast Asia, with danger all around, my worst nightmare since the age of 13 becoming all too real.

That worry was now history, so I could listen and debate "The Domino Theory" with the same kind of easy detachment I debated Existentialism.

The Civil Rights Movement was something else again. I couldn't ignore that. I had followed the movement closely. I watched and read everything I could about it. Nightly, I would sit, transfixed, by my little black and white television, fascinated by all of the many highlights: the bombings, the marches, the boycotts, the burning buses, the beatings and shootings, the awe inspiring speeches, and for the first time in my life, incredible, extraordinary people like James Baldwin, Malcolm X, Bayard Ruskin and Martin Luther King, Jr. unexpectedly began crowding my TV screen.

This was grand drama, better than anything I was reading in all the books I loved so much. I could see that right away. And it wasn't about who was right or who was wrong. It wasn't a question that these long-suffering black people, Americans who built the country and created its soundtrack, were noble, brave people fighting for long denied rights.

And, as all of this was unfolding day after day, year after year, somehow I felt left out, and that somehow I was not doing anything to help the movement and help my people.

***

In my small circle of friends before college, no one much talked about what was happening in the south. But the turning point for all of us was what happened in Birmingham, Alabama, and made us all pay more attention. In 1963, fire hoses and police dogs were set upon black demonstrators, as the Civil Rights Movement, led by Dr. Martin Luther King, Jr., once again filled my television screen.

A few days before that disgraceful event, when Birmingham's Police Commissioner Bull Connors turned loose his full city resources of policemen and firemen on those demonstrators (perhaps just as Martin Luther King had hoped he would in a classic "rope a dope" strategy)--I was talking to a middle aged white woman who had come over from England as a young child, and who now worked as a clerk on the same floor that I worked on at Robert Hall. She was telling me how much she had enjoyed her recent trip through Alabama.

"The people are so friendly and happy," she informed me.

"I don't think the black folks down there are happy at all," I answered.

"Oh, no. Oh, no. You are wrong there. They were very happy when I was there."

A few weeks later, the shit hit the fan. The next morning, after viewing the debacle in Birmingham on the Nightly News, I ran over to this woman's desk the minute I hit the floor, not even bothering to hang my coat in the dressing room.

"You still think they are happy? You still think they are happy!" I practically yelled at her. She just looked back at me strangely, and said nothing.

***

I had listened over the years with growing admiration to Malcolm X, and once seriously thought about becoming a Black Muslim. I once again discovered, after my tentative decision to go ahead with my idea to join the

Nation of Islam, that my inner personality has a propensity to become too over-heated, too extreme, and too ready to go to the mat (General Patton and I share three major things in common, I have learned, which I won't divulge, except for "Ok, put up your dukes, smart guy").

I couldn't walk around all day thinking about white people in such a hateful manner, no matter how much I felt they richly deserved it. So that idea was quickly banished from my head after only a few weeks, after I found myself glaring angrily, for no reason other than the fact that she was white, at a young woman on the No. 5 train to the Bronx, with nothing but red hot hatred and fury in my eyes and in my heart.

She had done nothing to me. I knew that. After that, I just didn't like the way hate made me feel. It just didn't wear well, no matter how hard I tried to make it fit.

***

1965 was the year that Malcolm X was murdered, while I was sitting in classrooms at NYU. But the epic civil rights battles in the nation continued. I wanted more than anything else to be involved in the struggle. I felt that I could use the great intelligence that I now was so sure of, and now held closely, to help black people, or Negros, as we were known then.

In a few years, I found an outlet.

***

I can still remember, as if it was yesterday, the day the world changed for me forever. I was sitting in the audience watching a group of black panelists discuss the Civil Rights Movement and where it was headed. It was 1967 and a panel discussion was being held at the Washington Square Campus of New York University. Here, on this stage, I watched for the first time in my life, highly educated, articulate, intelligent, committed black people.

One person in particular stood out from the others. She was a young woman, a few years older than me, and, as the others spoke, for some reason, I watched her carefully. She just sat and listened with an almost languid look on her attractive face, almost as if she was tired, or her mind was elsewhere. Her name was Eleanor Holmes Norton. She later became the Congressional Representative from the District of Columbia, among other important positions she held during her great career.

She did an incredible thing for me that afternoon.

As her turn to speak came, and she began her articulate speech, her entire being became alive in a way I had never witnessed before.

She had hope. She saw brotherhood. She saw an America where all races could love each other, and share what we had. I don't remember what exact words she used that afternoon, but whatever they were, the young, passionate Ms. Norton filled in me a new sense of direction and purpose. I now wanted to know people like her. I wanted desperately to be a part of whatever it was that so animated her with such conviction.

***

The same day that I was so turned on by the young, passionate Eleanor Holmes Norton, someone had passed out a flyer for a meeting that was going to be held on campus for a new black organization.

There was one other black person in my evening Associate Arts program. She looked a lot like my mother: fair-skinned, elegant and middle aged, but that is where the two parted company. My uneducated mother may have long harbored upper class dreams as the offspring of the most upper class black family in Northern Virginia, as well as being the nanny for several of the richest people in America, but they were kept in check by a grim reality, only occasionally flaring up in moments of downright disgust at the lower order.

She had to work hard in an overbearing, unforgiving New York City, just to keep herself and her four children afloat, without a man to help her (thank god she loved leaving the house five days a week, sometimes with snow piled so high I often wondered if she was going to come back. Sitting around waiting for something good to happen was not her style. I think this is how I picked up my love for work and a sense of purpose).

This woman, my classmate at NYU was a married, upper-class woman, just like her Jewish counterparts.

So where were the blacks?

A flyer offered promise. The first meeting was upstairs at the Loeb Student Center and the person who called it to order was a bright young law student by the name of Jimmy Carroll. My brother Rob had by now enrolled in the same program, only going for an AA in business, not the Liberal Arts section I was enrolled in. He had just finished serving four years in the Marines. (I was the wimp that joined the sissy-ass Army). I used my connection with the crooner, John O'Neal, to land him a job at the university.

I took Rob to that first meeting. I was very excited by the opportunity to meet other black people near my age, and I offered all kinds of ideas and suggestions. We named ourselves The Black American Student Association (BASA) of New York University.

We were black now, not Negroes. Stokely Carmichael, Chairman of The Student Non-violent Coordinating Committee (SNCC), had seen to that when he yelled "black power!" to the cameras at the continuation of the James Meredith march against fear. Mr. Meredith was shot afterwards in the back by a cowardly white man hiding in the bushes alongside a country road in Mississippi.

This BASA was soon going to put a stop to that kind of nonsense! In fact, we were going to do all kinds of wonderful things, including saving black people from the evil grip of white people. Still, I couldn't help noticing as we left the meeting, that all of us were able to fit into one elevator. Was this the entire black student body at NYU? If so, the first thing we needed to do was to save ourselves! It was clear that we had to find a way to bring more black students on campus.

***

On the subway back to the Bronx, I talked Rob's head off, still excited.

I quickly threw myself into this new organization. To put myself back on the couch, I have long seen a clear pattern to my behavior. I am clearly a joiner, despite all the bad names some people call me for being so inner driven. It is clear to me that I am not a loner, but someone who loves having many friends. My first job, at the age of ten, was delivering newspapers when I was living at The Home in Buffalo. It gave me a chance to meet people without the watchful eyes of Mrs. Thompson. The Home also had countless, sometimes deeply disturbed children coming and going. The Bad Boys of the Edenwald Enchanters provided an incredible male bonding that could only be experienced in an environment like I experienced as a teenager in the Third Armored Division. The Associate in Arts Program at NYU and then BASA--were all highly organized activities, with a complicated array of rules, taboos, rituals and pecking orders—and very defined individuals.

With BASA, I was just joining another gang, albeit a much smaller one than the ones I had been accustomed to.

***

Jimmy Carroll, the student who was the founding voice behind BASA, was a very serious young man, indeed. Then, he was thin, handsome, with light-brown skin and "good hair." He was from Queens, had successfully graduated both from high school and college, and was now a student at a prestigious law school, with only two other blacks.

Growing up, Queens, to those of us living in the Bronx, was a middle-class suburb, and the blacks who lived there were considered hopeless snobs.

Jimmy was a first year law student at NYU. He was no snob. In fact, he was very committed to the movement to help black people, much more than I was in 1967. He reminds me now of a much more fun Hillary Clinton, always on point.

Together, we began exploring the new, exciting world of black power. It made perfect sense for Jimmy, more so than me. College students—because of the Civil Rights Movement, the Vietnam War, and the ever lurking draft—were now center stage. Because of their sheer numbers, the Baby Boomers, of which I was merely on the cusp, now had a loud, growing, powerful voice; perhaps the first, and last time, young people in this age group would be able to have that much influence on the world scene.

The first thing Jimmy and I did was to start a newspaper, *The Faith*, which was my first tme in charge of an editorial product. We also started forming alliances with black students at City College, St. Johns and Columbia. In many ways, for me, this was the Enchanters all over again!

One bit of real excitement came when we visited Newark, New Jersey. That was the summer of 1967, right in the middle of the period known as the "long hot summers," when race riots were now commonplace. A race riot had recently occurred in Newark, killing 23 people and injuring 725 others. Black nationalists, like Newark native Amiri Baraka, called a Newark Black Power Conference, and leading figures in the new movement had been invited.

This would be our first opportunity to hang out with the big boys, so to speak.

The large auditorium that served as the main venue for the conference was packed with nationalists, and the atmosphere was fully charged. Cries of revolution were in the air. Jimmy excused himself after a while to go to the restroom.

A wild-eyed looking black man, wearing the white collar of a preacher, suddenly stood up and yelled, "And we have to get guns. We need to find all the guns we can find. Then we will show them they can't mess with us any longer!"

He was greeted with loud applause.

I was eager to get into the act, and have my voice heard. After all, wasn't that why I was there?

"Wait a minute. What's with all this gun stuff? Where the hell are you going to get enough guns to fight the United States army?" I said, dismissing the crazed looking preacher out of hand.

One by one, speaker after speaker rose. One said, "What we don't need are people like that guy in the red shirt. When the time comes, we will have to deal with people like that, as well."

Another said, "And that guy in the red shirt is the kind of nigger that have kept us down. But we know what to do with niggers like that, don't we, don't we?"

And the preacher himself said, staring directly at me, "Yes, we're going to get our guns; yes, we are going to arm ourselves; yes, we will take care of both the man and certain kinds of niggers who still think we should be licking the white man's boots!"

And all of this to loud approval from the overflowing crowd.

By this time, Jimmy had come back into the room.

"Who's this guy in the red shirt everybody seems to hate so much?" he whispered to me.

I pointed to my red shirt.

"Get the fuck out of here! Well, what the hell did you say?"

"Not much, but I think we need to get the fuck out of here," I answered, sensing that if I stayed I could become the stand-in for anyone this crowd had ever hated.

We left the auditorium, with me feeling little, sharp daggers in my back as we exited. Once again, I was the "little nigger who always had something to say."

This time, there was no mean, scary, big brother to hide behind.

***

On a more practical level, back in the relative safety of NYU, BASA was still faced with what could we do to help the cause. We tried raising funds for a scholarship for some lucky kid to attend college. One of our more cynical members asked the question: "This sounds like a lot of dances, dinners and parties to me, the great Negro fundraiser. Besides, what good is one little scholarship? How is that going to liberate black people?"

How indeed!

I knew it wasn't much. Jimmy and I both agreed that when you looked at the larger picture, something big had to happen. And that something big happened soon enough. Less than a year later, in April 1968, Dr. Martin Luther King was shot to death in Memphis.

***

I could not believe what had happened that night. I had been out drinking with some of the old gang from Robert Hall at a little dingy bar on 35th Street and Seventh Avenue. My marriage by this time had disintegrated, mainly because my wife had married one man, and right before her eyes, found he had transformed into someone she didn't know, a strangely driven man, totally lost in his world of conflict, glory and liberation, a total stranger. She had seen me almost have a nervous breakdown, having burst into deep, loud sobs a day after JFK was killed, the first time I had ever cried because of someone's death.

What was she to think of me? We had nothing left to talk about, and it was only a matter of time before I would be forced to leave our apartment in the projects.

The night of King's death I arrived home dead drunk.

"They shot him," she informed me, as I stumbled through the door.

"Shot who?" I muttered, collapsing on the couch.

"King!" I thought I heard her say, as I passed out from the drink, "They shot King!"

The next morning I was still lying on the couch. My wife had not even bothered to try and wake me to put me in bed. She said something about King getting shot, I thought, trying to remember what happened the night before. I got up. My wife and two kids were still sleeping. I wanted to avoid her, so I quickly washed and headed out of the door back down to NYU. The headlines in the papers told me the entire story. The air was so tense, it seemed as if you could cut it with a knife. Armed soldiers stood ready at subway stop after subway stop.

NYU seemed strangely deserted when I finally arrived and had officially closed down for the day. None of the members of BASA were around. I walked into the cafeteria at the Leob Student Center, and there I found only my friend Jimmy Carroll and an exchange student from Haiti. They were sitting at a table with a small portable typewriter, busily working on a document.

I joined them and together we drew up a series of "non-negotiable" demands which we were going to present to the entire student body at NYU, as they had all been called together because of the assassination. When the administration turned to him for help, Jimmy was smart enough to realize he had a real opportunity in his hands and I was glad as hell that I had showed up to help him craft the final product.

Under the bold headline, THE NON-NEGOTIABLE DEMANDS OF THE AD HOC BLACK STUDENT ASSOCIATION, the three of us demanded a black student center, a black Institute of African-American Affairs, a black studies program, and more black students on campus. Also, that a Martin

Luther King Scholarship fund be set up to help pay the tuition of these new recruits.

I, Jimmy Carroll, and our friend from Haiti, marched into the crowded auditorium carrying our document, with a few to pass out, and walked up to the front of the room. All eyes were on us. We had not planned it as such, but it was clear that we were going to play good cop, bad cop with these people.

I had on dark, Rap Brown sunglasses, jeans, and a newly grown, huge Afro.

I stood next to Jimmy, my arms folded, trying to look as mean as I could, while copying the pose of my new heroes in the black power movement. Jimmy, looking middle-class and as always, sporting a tie, read our demands calmly, but forcefully.

After he finished, someone asked a question. Jimmy was about to answer when I angrily grabbed the mike out of his hands. "You don't need to answer the questions of these racist motherfucking killers!" I said, forcefully. "Let's just get the fuck out of here. They have our demands. They know what we want."

I stared long and hard at the people in the audience, revealing little behind my dark shades. And I knew that they knew that I felt that they were now beneath hatred, and that I only felt contempt for them, and their hateful, fascist system that had murdered Dr. King.

They were all liars, murderers and blood-suckers and they knew it!

I put the mike back into its holder, and Jimmy, the young man from Haiti and I dramatically walked down the aisle and out of the large auditorium.

On the way out, I heard a woman crying softly. I also heard another woman say, her voice filled with grief and hurt, "see what you did, you scared the black students away. Why did you do have to do that?"

In the end, every single demand that we had listed, was met by the university, and most are still in place, as I write this. Quietly, both Jimmy and I, and perhaps the exchange student from Haiti, realized that perhaps we had made a real contribution to the movement, and had done something to help black people, and help the nation.

For me, the main lesson I took from what happened that day is that the key to a fruitful life is to show up when needed most.

I received one of the first Martin Luther King Scholarship Awards we had proposed in our demands, and because of that, along with the new GI bill due to the war in Vietnam, I was finally able to transfer full time.

I obviously did not become President of the United States, but I did receive a degree in journalism in 1971.

***

I was the pre-teen, honorary Italian attending Sunday Mass with my friends in the Upper Bronx, and having a pizza afterward; I was the highly sensual teenager, madly in love with his beautiful mother; I was a proud member of the tragic, doomed, bad boys of the mighty Edenwald Enchanters; I stood next to a young Puerto Rican as he shot to death another young man; I was kicked out of high school at sixteen; I was the Black Power militant with the dark shades and huge Afro at NYU; and, I slept with Elvis.

If I wasn't an American, then the elites were right; there was no such thing.

***

Chapter Eleven, Big Man on Campus

I was shown the door after my first year of high school, so two years later I joined the Army at the age of eighteen and served with Elvis. I decided soon after my service, as I slowly began to think of myself as a genius, especially since the Army said I had a IQ of 149, that I could become President of the USA because of my love for President Kennedy, who always seemed to be talking directly to me—if only I could get a law degree like him.

By this time, all my friends began to see me as somewhat strange. One friend even laughed in my face at the news that I wanted to be President.

"Nigger, are you crazy! You don't even have a high school diploma."

Yet the laughter soon stopped two years later when I had not only a GED high school diploma, but also was now a student at NYU, way before Affirmative Action. I had skipped high school and went straight to college.   Who does that! I must be the genius I now thought I was

In addition, I started my journalism career at NYU by starting a student newspaper, *The Faith.* And at 25, I started a national magazine, *Black Creation: A Quarterly of Black Arts and Letters,* now proudly in the new African American Museum in Washington; and, for most of my stay at NYU, I was a Big Man on Campus. And, best of all, I have made the history books (55 books and counting) just by *Black Creation* alone.

All of this was because I never allowed others to tell me what I could or couldn't do. I had a funny kind of reasoning for my attitude. What I knew from American history was that it was the Northern Europeans that prevented blacks from being free because they had guns, bombs and the rope, and didn't mind using them against any black they disliked.

My favorite example is what happened to a young black woman, Ida B. Wells, who was born a slave. She co-owned a newspaper, the *Memphis Free Speech* in the 1890s, and spoke out against lynching and racial injustice. For her efforts her house was set upon by a white mob one night, was bombed and burned to the ground, and her precious printing press was destroyed.

Ida B. Wells could have also been destroyed just like her printing press and house, but just happened to be out of town in New York City. After that, she left Memphis, never to return.

Well, all that was gone, hopefully never to become a part of American history again, thanks to the Civil Rights Movement. We were now free, all of us, blacks and whites, after 277 years of slavery, and another 100 years of part-time slavery, on this soil called America.

So, why pay any attention to the guilt tripping and name calling and psychological warfare of the black Nationalists and Eastern Europeans at NYU trying to keep me in my place, because in my odd mind; if no one was going to physically harm me, who cares what they think about me?

I also first learned at NYU the stark details of the narrative which is imprinted in the mind of almost every black American. I call it the quiet voice from the grave. But it was not the voices of long-dead black relatives that were whispering comforting things to them, but the low, almost imperceptible voice of the Slave Master that said over and over, "Know your place because you will never live a moment of your life without your fear of me."

But that old wrinkled, white motherfucker didn't scare me, like it did the Affirmative Action black students that came to NYU right after the killing of Martin Luther King. I was a blank slate and was too unschooled to even know that I was not supposed to just waltz into NYU and say, "Hi gang, I'm here!" or do all the other things I was now doing, because I was poor, black and male. In addition, whoever heard of someone that did so well, that didn't have a wise preacher, or pushy parents, or civil rights leaders, or good friends egging him on?

I tried to tell my fellow students, black and white, that only my own naive mind said that I could be anything I wanted to be. Also, I had a profoundly cool, rational mind. So, because of the two, only I could tell me what was real. What I didn't tell them that there was a cost to be had for this behavior. The first was that my lovely young wife finally dumped me and threw my stuff and my black ass out the door shortly after I became a student at NYU. She thought I had ice water for blood.

I didn't blame her. She had married one man, and woke up one morning with someone strange, and suddenly driven. She didn't know what to think of this, and all I could say to her that game changing morning is, "I got the spirit!"

I made little sense that morning and weeks after because I now felt a strange sense of energy I had never felt before, and which has never left me—which frightened her to death but made me feel invincible.

The blank slate. I have nothing to protect me. Why would someone lie to me?

In other words, I did not realize the value of lying and bullshitting. When I took the entrance exam at NYU, I scored in the top 7 percent. I knew a lot about so much. What I didn't know was human nature. You can't get that from a book, but at the dinner table, listening to your folks.

At NYU, most of what I was taught as a journalism major was lying to protect an interest or a group that the Professors cared deeply about.

They taught me the basic mechanics of journalism, which was well taught, indeed, and has served me well in my great career. No doubt about it. But telling us that we're about to enter America journalism was the biggest lie going. I found out that there was no such thing as American journalism.

What I found was three kinds of journalism: Racial journalism, Tribal journalism, and most clever of all, Tribal journalism masquerading as Racial journalism. What I also found when I left NYU was a lot of loneliness and a lot of lying.

Chapter Twelve, Black Creation

After I graduated from NYU in 1971 with my well-earned degree, a yearning came over me. I wanted to get out of New York to see the country, so I could live like the American I was. At that time, I was living with my girlfriend, a smart, curious, beautiful young blond who called herself a "Scan." She was half Swedish and half Norwegian. She called herself that because New York is perhaps the most tribal city in America, so she had to call herself something, and she was clearly 100 percent Scandinavian.

She would also get very pissed off at me for my saying I was not a minority, as she would sometimes call me. I was an American, I explained to her, and we Americans were the majority in this country.

She would huff and puff and almost turn red, but to no avail.

"You're too much," she would finally say

She was right. Nobody was going to call me a minority and get away with it. And, please, I quietly suggested to her, not wanting to ruin the wonderful sex life we had, don't ever call me an immigrant.

I sometimes drove her crazy, but she loved wrapping her warm arms around me at night as we made love. And, I love her for it—the polemics where quickly forgotten.

We had first met in our Sophomore year at NYU, and she moved in with me, in my small one-bedroom in Chelsea that same summer. She was from New England and was the only blonde I ever saw on campus, mainly because at that time NYU was 95 percent Jewish.

Some black students used to call NYU, NYJEW.

In a funny way, my girlfriend and I both stuck out. I was one of the few blacks in the journalism department, and she was perhaps the only non-Jewish woman in it; furthermore, the only real blonde in the entire school.

She got an internship at *Newsday* in our Junior year, the same year I started *Black Creation,* and because of her dance background, started covering dance performances, which won her a national journalism student award for best arts commentary.

We played footsie at the award ceremony for her, as our chair, Professor M.L. Stein, sang her praises. These days we would be called a power couple, but back then we had to keep our relationship quiet. Professor Stein had no idea what we were doing as he droned on.

***

The Civil Rights Movement had quieted down, as well as the Vietnam War, as we neared the end of our stay at NYU. As for me, I thought that the Civil Rights Movement was going to destroy Apartheid, and one could live anywhere they wanted, marry anyone they wanted, get any job they could do as well as anyone else.

In other words, blacks should now be full-fledged Americans, especially because we had been here since the 1630's, not to mention the blacks that came with the Spanish a hundred years before the English and French ever step foot in the new world.

But that was not to be the case. Starting in the late 60s a huge backlash occurred after black males and white women started dating in large numbers for the first time in our history. By the time we were in our last year at NYU, I remember reading an item in an article written by a black woman in the new *Essence* magazine. The writer vehemently denounced interracial couples and added that, "we should attack these people when we see them on the streets."

My beautiful, curious, blonde girlfriend, whose name I will not use, was perhaps the whitest woman not just at NYU but in New York City. In fact, a good friend of mine said to me with a serious face, "Fred, I don't mind you having a white girlfriend, but do you have to go out with the whitest woman in town?"

I broke out laughing, not just for what he said but his serious face when saying it.

But, he was right. New Yorkers, black and white, watched our every move. One Sunday morning we opened the weekend version of the *New York Post* and there was a shot of us riding our bikes in Washington Square Park. The photographer shot us from behind, but it was us all right. There was nowhere for us to hide as we walked the streets of the Village.

Not many beautiful "Scans" and handsome black men to speak of in 1971 walking the streets of New York City. No wonder that writer at

Essence wanted to chase us out of town. We were setting a bad example.

***

We both immediately found good jobs when we graduated. She started working as an Assistant Editor for a political magazine called *Change.* The day we received our diploma at Town Hall, I left the ceremony still wearing my cap and gown and walked over to the office of *Essence* magazine, where I was now the Managing Editor. I stuck my cap and gown in my desk drawer and began my job at the magazine.

Yes, the same magazine that recently thought that my bright, sexy girlfriend and I should be attacked on the streets just for walking together.

I was recruited for this job by the well-known poet, Nikki Giovanni, who was a good friend, and she was also the friend of the new editor of *Essence*, Ida Lewis.

Nikki had already done something for me that changed my life, forever.

On the weekends I would often go over to her apartment on 93rd Street, right off Columbus, in Manhattan, and chat a little. This one Saturday I was in a deep funk. When I started as a night student at NYU, it was 1966. It wasn't until 1968 that I was finally able to go full time. This was now 1970, and I was sick and tired of school. I wanted action, not classrooms or peer pressure. I was on the verge of quitting.

Nikki would have none of it. "There is nothing like finishing something. Take my word for it. Keep that in mind," she said, after insisting that my leaving school was a bad idea. Her wise advice was just what I wanted to hear, and my funk went away just like that.

***

>

I had also been recruited for a job at the new black business magazine, Earl Graves' *Black Enterprise*,but I didn't take it.

All this recruiting was for two reasons. First, it was still a few years before the first batch of black Affirmative Action students were to graduate from many colleges and universities around the country, as they also had put into place the same kind of programs for black students as was done at NYU. So, I was still one of the few blacks in New York with a degree from a prestigious school like NYU.

What also helped was the great unsung initiative to help blacks, President Richard Nixon's Black Capitalism. I am convinced that this great idea received little praise but much scorn because the so-called liberal media, which was really the largest tribal media in the country, hated Nixon with the same passion as they hate President Donald J. Trump. They weren't about to praise anything about Nixon and soon were able to run him out of office.

But Black Capitalism spawned many black-owned businesses, including *Essence* and *Black Enterprise* and other businesses that still exist today.

But the main reason why I was so sought after was because of the magazine I founded at NYU, *Black Creation: A Quarterly of Black Arts and Letters. Black Creation*, as I pointed out in my introduction, has put me in the history books, as well as a spot in the Smithsonian African American Museum in Washington.

I started the magazine in 1968 after a tiff with one of the students working with me on the black newspaper that I founded with law student James Carroll called *The Faith.*

When the Affirmative Action students started pouring into NYU, Jimmy and I were more than glad to see them. Several of them joined the newspaper, and, keeping with the spirit of the times, we abolished all titles and called ourselves a Collective.

This night we were working with the printers in a hot, noisy shop. This was the waning years of "hot type," where the letters were molded by melted lead. It was hot, dirty, heavy lifting. The white men doing the work dressed in t-shirts and had tattoos on their big arms. This kind of shop was no place for sissies or women. I had spent years working in the Garment Center nearby and felt right at home there with these men.

I had written for *The Faith* my first book review ever. The book was a collection of short stories by the South African writer, Alan Paton of *Cry, the Beloved Country* fame. It seemed to The Collective that I was overly sympathy to one of the white characters in one of the stories.

I was told by John Doe (I won't reveal his real name), the smart guy who I loved to debate with because he was so quick of mind, that they could not allow me to publish this review unless I change it.

"Are you kidding?"

"No."

The beast in me suddenly came out. "This is my fucking paper! You want to take this shit outside."

Who in the fuck died and left these Bozos in charge! The other members of The Collective stood behind John Doe. It was a Palace coup. I stormed out, shouting loudly, "fuck you, motherfuckers!"

But I soon cool down, mainly because I knew something. That something was that I doubted if The Collective would ever publish another issue. I was the one that made things happen, including bringing their sorry asses to NYU! I was wrong, however. They managed to get out one more. After that, *The Faith* was history

In 2009, John Doe contacted me on Facebook. The first thing I said to him was that he was responsible for my great career in journalism. That time in that loud, hot printer's shop was my never-again moment, which cause me to start *Black Creation* with no such thing as a Collective. I was in charge, period.

Thanks John Doe, I needed that.

What I did with *Black Creation*, was something that had never been done in black journalism before, or for that matter, after. It started out as a literary magazine for the black students at NYU. I tried to raise money for the magazine, which I saw in my mind. I even had the cover mentally in mind.

But it was slow going. I put on several debates and charged admission but that did not generate enough income.

One day I was in yet another of my deep funks and talking to one of the black students about the magazine. She said, "Look, we now have a Black Institute of African American Affairs, but Dr. Brown so far doesn't seem to know what to do next. You should go talk to him. I think he would back the magazine."

She was right. Dr. Roscoe C. Brown was the only black Ph.D. teaching at the university that I knew of. What he taught was physical education. The black students called him a "gym teacher." But there were things about Dr. Brown that they didn't know, and I didn't know until many years later. He was one of the famed, black Tuskegee Airmen in World War II, the first time in history that black American men could fly in the Army Air Corp. This was not the first time that black men flew in battle. In World War I, France allowed black men to fly for them.

And to top that, Dr. Brown was widely credited with being the first airman ever to shoot down one of the new Nazi's jet planes, they being the first nation on Earth to use such an awesome weapon.

When I found out about all this, I wondered why I never heard or read about the Tuskegee Airmen. Me, the bookworm, know-it-all. What also puzzled me was why Dr. Brown didn't talk about all of this to the black students, including me. Maybe they would have given him more respect then, rather than calling him "gym teacher."

At any rate, Dr. Brown jumped to the idea of the magazine. He immediately started telling me what he expected out of *Black Creation* and me. I stopped him in mid-sentence. I was not going to have another John Doe on my hands.

"Dr. Brown," I said, "I will run this magazine the way I want. All I want from you is an office and funds. It will be known as *Black Creation: A Quarterly of Black Arts and Letters, a Publication of The Institute of African American Affairs at NYU.* I have already filed a copyright in my name for the name of this magazine."

He smiled at me, almost, I sensed, in relief. "Good, good, it's all yours. Let's get started."

Again, thank you John Doe.

***

The major reasons I was so dedicated to creating such a magazine was because of what was happening in the black community nationwide. In addition to carrying a full load at NYU, I also had a family to help feed, which now included two small children, although I no longer lived with them but had moved back to my mother's house in the upper Bronx. I had the G.I. bill, thanks to the war in Vietnam. But I was no longer working for NYU. I need to make more money.

I brought myself a camera and became a reporter/photographer at Percy Sutton's *New York Courier* in Harlem. Pat Patterson, the writer I met while I was working for the James Farmer Congressional run in Bed-Sty, Brooklyn, was the Managing Editor.

What I saw covering events in Harlem and what I saw on college campuses in the entire city, was an enormous outpouring of black creativity. Black Americans were now going though one of the greatest changes in our history in this country. The Civil Rights Movement was over. A conservative backlash, as I have noted, was the *Spirit of the Times*. First came Black Power, then came The Black Consciousness Movement, then finally, The Black Arts Movement.

The Black Power Movement held a great interest to me because it spoke to blacks creating businesses and taking charge of their communities and stop whining to whites for everything. I had my doubts about the Black Consciousness Movement. I came from a mixed-race family as I pointed out in Book One. I also thought that the One Drop

Rule was a fairy tale. As I wrote in my first novel, *The Womanizer*, "Only a nation of morons could believe in something so stupid."

This didn't go over well with the new New York publishing crowd that by now had chased the old guard "white shoe" publishers and editors back to Connecticut where their WASP asses belonged. One Liberal (why they are called Liberals I will never know) literary agent said to me after reading my novel and my first book of essays, *The Rejected American,* "Nobody in this town is going to publish you. You need to learn how to write the way we want or we will never allow you to be published in this country."

It was the "we" that I noted most. In the end, I laughed in her face. She was an immigrant, I was an American. No way on God's good earth was her "we" going to tell me what to think or write. The nerve!

That little polemic was an aside. What I found out years later, when DNA results became all the rage, that I was quite correct when I said I was not an African, but an American. I am 70 percent Yoruba, 5 percent Bushman of the Kalahari, 19 per cent Northern European (Germany, Denmark, Finland), 5 per cent Native American and 1.3 percent Neanderthal. You are not going to get more American than that!

But back to my narrative, the Black Nationalists and the so-called Liberals thought The Black Consciousness Movement was a great idea. Think black, be black. You were Africans, not Americans, and don't ever forget it, and stay the hell away from white people. Especially white women.

This was easy to do for the so-called Liberals. Their DNA goes back unbroken for over five thousand years.

Those black Americans, which are many, that have only DNA from Africa, which goes back unbroken since the coming of human beings, have a real point when they say being blacks is not just a word, but a total inner being. I have always acknowledged that.

But what about black Americans like me? (And there are plenty of us as well. In fact, we might just be the majority.) Additionally, what made black American burst on the world stage was how pure Africans and mixed-race blacks made common cause, mainly because of the One Drop Rule.

It was mixed-race people like Booker T. Washington, Frederick Douglass, W.E.B. Du Bois and the grand Black Nationalist of all, the mixed race Malcolm X, with his light brown eyes, red hair, and famous quote: "I hate the white blood running through my vines that was put there by a white rapist"—that brought us to the position we now have.

Brazil has the largest black population in the New World. They also have a large mixed-race population. Together, they are the majority in that country. But they have absolutely no real power, because blacks and mixed-race people view each other separately.

So, to me, The Black Consciousness Movement was a movement that was going to fracture the unity that we had until then. That's why I never use the words African-American. It was something that the so-called Liberals foisted on us, thinking that we will never find out how one day we were black Americans and the next we were all Africans.

But the Black Arts Movement was something totally different. It was unlike the famous Harlem Renaissance in almost every way. The Harlem Renaissance took place in the 1920s and was mainly a literary, jazz and theatre movement in Harlem. In addition, this was also the first time in New York City history that Uptown met Downtown.

This was the jazz age. Folks wanted to forget about the most brutal war ever, followed by the horrific, worldwide outbreak of the deadly Spanish Flu. Now, Wall Street was booming, nightlife was filled with white people dancing the night away in hideaway speakeasys filled with bootleg whiskey, beautiful showgirls and red-hot black jazz, and no greater place to find all of this merriment and carrying on was black Harlem.

In addition, white gay men like Carl Van Vechten, who was the Theater Editor for *Vanity Fair Magazine*, along with several other important gay magazine critics, befriended people like the great Langston Hughes and other black gay men, who wrote, or sang, or worked as actors and even directors, and wrote about them in their glossy magazines and gave the name Harlem to the world.

But the Black Arts Movement? One thing that made it different was the fact that it was nationwide and not just centered in New York. From San Francisco, to Boston, to Atlanta, to New Orleans, to Chicago, to Los Angeles, to all black New York—the Black Arts Movement was bursting with new-found raw creative energy.

In addition, being the flagship of the movement did not have a literary component. This was a performance-based movement. The literary aspect of it was the spoken word, not words on paper. Poetry reading were held all over, and small clubs and large 200-seat spaces were packed with eager listeners.

In addition, theatre and dance company started springing up all over the country, and here in New York, The Dance Theatre of Harlem, Alvin Ailey, The Negro Ensemble Company, The New Lafayette Theatre quickly became international sensations.

Jazz and the Visual Arts, including paintings and creative photography, joined in as well.

I knew I had to capture all of this. And this we did in *Black Creation*. It is also why I am in so many history books. Historians have started looking back at this time of great creativity in the same way that they have looked back on the Lost Generation and the Harlem Renaissance.

The main problem for these historians has been the fact that the white community covered little of this. In fact, many whites thought that the Black Arts Movement was anti-white, especially because of firebrand poets like Amiri Baraka, formerly Leroi Jones, who was also seen as the leader of the Black Arts Movement and who often used violent rhetoric directed at whites.

So, because of this *Black Creation* was one of the few outlets that covered all of this. I did not just cover New York City, but had correspondents in cities across the country.

It wasn't until the internet age began that I discovered just how important *Black Creation* is to historians. I had no idea and was totally amazed as the books started piling up, as historians started recognizing that this was one of the most vivant, creative periods in American history, and I was right there to record most of it. I also discovered that much of what I wrote in the magazine has been republished

For example, The University Press of Mississippi Literary Conversation Series published *Conversations with Ernest Gaines*, *Conversations with Albert Murray* and *Conversations with John A. Williams*. In each book I had the first conversation. All three came out of *Black Creation*. The Gaines book and the Albert Murray book was published before the internet. No one contacted me for my permission. They had no means to contact me because I was living first in Los Angeles and then San Francisco. It was only the last book, *Conversations with John A. Williams,* published in 2018, in which the editor of the book asked my permission.

In addition, I found several other textbooks that had entire chapters on *Black Creation* and me. I especially loved the way they threw the word "brilliant" around. Part of the reason why I didn't know about all of

this was because I was reading history books written by black writers.
Only one black historian, Houston Baker, mentioned *Black Creation*.

The basic problem I have with black historians is the fact that they consider the Civil Rights Movement black history. It is just a segment, albeit, perhaps the most important segment of black history here in America, but there is so much more. That is why *Black Creation* is loved by the historians: because I documented the so much more.

I often wonder what my inner self would have been if I had known about what was going on. One of the things the book agents said to me when I was trying to find a publisher was that I never did anything, and I was now in my 50s trying to become a writer?

My hat was in my hands and my spirits low as I was chastened time after time, unknowingly not knowing that I was a giant among giants, not the Joe Nobody the agents thought me to be.

The Black Arts Movement started in 1968 and ended in 1973. And, it was time for me to encounter America.

Chapter Thirteen: Seeing America

The ongoing, nonstop harassments were getting to both of us.

Walking out the door, although we lived in the liberal 70s, on the Upper

West Side, we didn't know what to expect. If we were in the supermarket together, there may be an angry black woman glaring at us. If we walked

down the street, especially at night, there was the chance that white men

would get into the act and would shout nasty words at us as they rode by

in a car.

I quickly left *Essence* after Ida Lewis was fired but continued to run

Black Creation. I also started working for the first black public relations

firm, Jim Booker and Associates, on Madison Avenue. Interesting

enough, my girlfriend's magazine was only a few blocks from my office.

After long conversations, my girlfriend and I decided to move to

California. We had heard so much about San Francisco and Berkeley

that we decided to move to the Bay Area. Also, for me, the second

largest market I had for *Black Creation* was the Bay Area. I could tell

from that I was already well known there.

I told Jim Booker that I was planning on moving. I made a deal with

him that he not pay me each week but hold my salary for the next two

month and give it to me in a lump sum. Although he was sorry to see me

go, he agreed. He absolutely loved the profiles, press releases and

features that I churn out for our clients.

My thinking was that I still had my salary from the Institute of African

American Affairs at NYU, which would last as long as I was still running the magazine, no matter where I was. Plus, my girlfriend had a well-paying job and was not a spendthrift, so, when we left for The Bay Area, we were loaded with dough.

I also learned, to my surprise, that my girlfriend was afraid of flying, so we decided to take Amtrak. Little did I know that this would be the first of countless trips over the years, back and forth, from Los Angeles to New York, and from New York to the Bay Area. The night before we left, we went to see the Joffrey Ballet at Lincoln Center. This was the same night that the Vietnam War ended.

At the curtain call, the dancers got loud curtain call after curtain call. It was nothing I had ever seen before. The audience would not let them leave the stage.

For me, after seeing so many dance concerts, thanks to my girlfriend and our free, best seats in the house press tickets—this was just a so, so show. But, I sensed that this out pouring of sheer emotion had little to do with the dance concert, as good as it was, but was a shout out to the long, contentious war that few wanted and that changed America almost beyond recognition; and the folks at the concert at the Lincoln Center were overjoyed that it was finally brought to an end.

***

We spent most of our time in the observation car on our way west, watching our America pass slowly by, especially after as we left Chicago and after we had changed to the larger, more comfortable cross-country train, the California Zephyr.

The landscape slowly emptied of people. From New York to Chicago there was human life everywhere, but after Illinois, where did all the people go? At NYU, the talk, after all the loud noise of the Civil Rights Movement and the War in Vietnam, was about the danger of over population. But, how could that be, now that I am seeing this wide-open country for the first time? If anything, this country seemed under populated.

I saw a lot of cows, and surprisingly, many short-tailed deer grazing among the cattle. You could tell that the deer were different in kind than the cows. The fat cows grazed lazily, contentedly, rarely taking their eyes off the ground.

The deer were lean, skittish, uptight, always looking up and around, their short tails jerking nervously around, appearing as if they were prepared to quickly run off, which they occasionally did in short bursts, only to stop and start their nervous grazing again.

The fat, lazy cows paid them or anything else little mind and only concentrated on the grass in front of their noses. But I knew that it was just that skittishness that kept these trim, freedom loving deer off someone's dinner plate, and that was why they were still thriving in the new world.

Now and then I caught a glimpse of a smart, wily coyote, with large pointed ears, its head pointed downward, occasionally looking over its shoulders, the outline of its distinctly curved back even recognizable to a big city type such as I.

As it stealthily stalked its next victim, paying little attention to the large train passing by, I knew that was no dog.

This country was truly amazing! Full of surprise after surprise. Wily coyotes! Nervous deer! What next, buffalo, cowboys and Indians? I was amazed as a small group of young black kids waved vigorously at the train as we passed through their tiny little town in the middle of nowhere. What were they doing out here? Blacks were not supposed to live this far west with its miles and miles of empty space!

In some of the far-Western states like Utah, Nevada and Wyoming, we would travel for hours and hours and not see any sign of life, not even a telephone pole. For someone who had spent most of his life in two big, teeming old world cities like Buffalo and New York City, this was beyond strange.

As America unfolded itself before us my girlfriend was as curious as I. She rarely took her eyes off the swiftly passing landscape as we passed through yet another little speck on the map. With her face pressed against the train window, her mouth slightly open and her eyes following whatever it was that had caught her fancy at that moment, it wasn't a passive stare but an engaged, actively aggressive stare.

The mountain state of Colorado really reached into our car and grabbed both of us by the throat as we passed over the mightily Rockies. Our heavily straining train sometimes seemed ready to fail us as we seemed to be barely hanging onto to the top of the world. The magnificent Rockies were still covered with patches of snow the higher we got. They would soon help water most of the west.

I watched as a high flying, large bird glided slowly and effortlessly by, its large wingspan stretched widely to capture the warm updrafts from the valleys below.

"Must be a bald eagle," I said to my girlfriend, not knowing what that big black bird really was, but hoping that it was indeed a bald eagle. This would have been a far greater experience than if it was just a plain old crow.

My girlfriend later informed me, after I continued to go on and on about seeing a bald eagle, that bald eagles are not all black but have a distinct white crown and white feet.

"Sorry. Maybe it was a crow," she said, still staring out of the window. "Or, maybe a raven, or whatever they call it so far out here, but it certainly was *not* a bald eagle."

But, so what, know-it-all, smarty pants? As far as I was concerned, it was a bald eagle and would remain so in my memories of that first trip west. So there.

Finally, we reached Reno after experiencing the bleak moonscape of the Nevada desert. There was a huge banner welcoming us to, "The Biggest Little City in the World." We were also at the foot of the Sierra Nevada mountains. While not as mighty as the Rockies, nevertheless they gave many pioneers much sorrow. For example, the ill-fated Donner: They were a group of pioneers that set out for California in a wagon train in May,1846. They were delayed by a series of mishaps and mistakes and spent the winter of 1846–47 snowbound in the Sierra Nevada. Some of the pioneers resorted to cannibalism to survive.

We set out at the end of June, and unlike the Donner party, we came to the same place, but it only took us three days, and the heavy snow was all but gone. As we started reaching the peak, we had listened to a history of the rail line and the many people that lost life and limb making it happen.

"Look down to the right," the recording said, "If you look hard enough you can see down to where the Donner Party stayed for the winter."

The recording also paid homage to a statue of a Chinese worker. From 1864 to the finishing of the line over the mountains to Reno in 1868, it was the Chinese the bore the most important role in finishing the work on the line.

Finally, the earth flattened, and we were in the heart of California. A new adventure was about to unfold.

9 781929 188338